THE
MITZVAH
OF HEALING

An Anthology of Jewish Texts,
Meditations, Essays,
Personal Stories, and Rituals

Edited by

RABBI HARA E. PERSON

Women of Reform Judaism/UAHC Press
New York, New York

Library of Congress Cataloging-in-Publication Data

The mitzvah of healing : an anthology of Jewish texts, meditations,
  essays, personal stories, and rituals / edited by Hara E. Person.
    p. cm.
  Includes index.
  ISBN 0-8074-0856-5 (pbk. : alk. paper)
  1. Healing—Religious aspects—Judaism.   2. Spiritual healing.
  3. Judaism—Prayer-books and devotions.   4. Judaism—Customs
  and practices.   I. Person, Hara.

BM538.H43M57 2003
296.7--dc21   2002042980

Contents

Foreword

DEBBIE FRIEDMAN

When I lived in Chicago, I got a phone call on a Shabbat morning from a professor with whom I was studying. He was Orthodox. He asked me if I would mind driving him to the hospital, as he was legally blind. His wife was ill, and he wanted to spend the day with her. For him, there was no question as to where he needed to be. For him, the mitzvah of *bikur cholim,* "visiting the sick," took priority over the laws of Shabbat or, for that matter, anything else in his life.

Bikur cholim includes the opportunity for visiting the sick, praying for the sick, and all things connected to caring for those who are ill. It extends beyond the physical realm, touching the heart and soul of the person in need of healing.

The Mitzvah of Healing presents us with the opportunity to participate in healing ourselves and others. The process of healing is not only about physical recovery, but about spiritual and emotional receptivity.

We both give and receive as we lead healing services, bring food and other necessities, and pray with people at their bedsides or privately. Someone who is recovering might be the beneficiary of our prayers, love, or friendship. We can be messengers of blessing and comfort to them.

Sometimes we stand alone with those in need, and sometimes we work with a team in our communities. We are always working in partnership with the Holy One. Our task is to perform *bikur cholim,* "caring for the sick," which will bring healing to the world and relieve the world of its pain and suffering.

Women of Reform Judaism, under the direction of Ellen Rosenberg, is a model for such acts of *g'milut chasadim,* "acts of loving-kindness." *The Mitzvah of Healing* is a guide for action. Using it, we are directed on a path of mitzvah, of fulfilling the obligations of caring for those who are ill.

May these words find their way into your hearts. May you be strengthened to bless those around you with courage to make all of our lives a blessing.

Acknowledgments

Special thanks are due to many people. This book originated as a project of Women of Reform Judaism (WRJ), and many people from WRJ helped with the gestation. It was Ellen Rosenberg who gave the first official go-ahead to this project and had the vision and flexibility necessary to ensure that this book would come into the world. Eve F. Roshevsky was there from the start with unwavering faith in this book, and did everything possible to help see it through to publication. Barbara Jayson collected the mass of textual materials that were selected and shaped into the present volume. Without their energy and dedication, and without the support of the whole WRJ staff and membership, there would be no *Mitzvah of Healing*.

Many others deserve special thanks as well. A debt of gratitude is owed to Debbie Friedman for her invaluable support and her contributions both in the form of her loving tribute at the beginning of the book and her own personal story of healing. The National Council of Jewish Women and Ma'yan must be thanked for use of their libraries. Rabbi Simkha Y. Weintraub, of the National Center for Jewish Healing in New York (NCJH), generously provided help and advice, as well as permission to include valuable publications of the center as well as his own texts and translations. Susie Kessler, also of NCJH, was tremendously helpful and supportive.

Once this book passed into the hands of the UAHC Press, it benefited greatly from the attention and care of some people who made important contributions. Ken Gesser was an enthusiastic supporter of this project from the beginning and welcomed it warmly into the Press. Liane Broido spent an incalculable number of hours tracking down permissions and preparing a final version of the manuscript for publication. Doug Barden, Michael Geller, and Michael Holzman of NFTB were helpful in trying to track down additional material, and their support in this project is greatly appreciated. Annie Belford Vernon searched for material with true devotion and found some important additions to the book. Debra Hirsch Corman treated this project with her usual dedication, and it is a far better book due to her care. However, it is not just the work that leads up to publication that counts. Thanks are also due, therefore, to Joel Eglash, for without his efforts none of what went into creating this book would matter.

Every effort has been made to contact copyright owners of previously published materials reprinted in *The Mitzvah of Healing*. The editor will be glad to hear from any authors whose materials have inadvertently been omitted from the following list, and to include full and proper acknowledgment in future editions.

RENNI S. ALTMAN: "*MiSheberach* for *Shalom Bayit*" by Rabbi Renni S. Altman. Reprinted by permission of Rabbi Renni S. Altman.

AMIT: "Can Prayer Heal?" by Erica Brown from *Amit Magazine*. Reprinted by permission of *Amit Magazine*. For more information: *amitmag@amitchildren.org* and *www.amitchildren.org*.

KAREN BENDER: "HIV Positive and AIDS" by Rabbi Karen Bender. Reprinted by permission of Rabbi Karen Bender.

SHERRY H. BLUMBERG: "Haggadah for Healing" by Dr. Sherry H. Blumberg from *The Outstretched Arm* 5, no. 2 (spring 1996), NCJH. Reprinted by permission of Dr. Sherry H. Blumberg.

NINA BETH CARDIN: "The Dew of Life" by Rabbi Nina Beth Cardin, from *The Outstretched Arm* 5, no. 1 (fall 1995), NCJH. Reprinted by permission of Rabbi Nina Beth Cardin.

CENTRAL CONFERENCE OF AMERICAN RABBIS: "On Recovery," "Upon Terminating a Pregnancy," and "After a Stillbirth or Upon the Death of a Young Child" from *On the Doorposts of Your House*, edited by

Rabbi Chaim Stern. Copyright © 1994 by the Central Conference of American Rabbis and used by permission.

CENTRAL SYNAGOGUE: "A Special Prayer in Time of Illness" from *Central Synagogue Healing Service.* Reprinted by permission of Central Synagogue.

NANCY FLAM: "The Jewish Way of Healing" by Rabbi Nancy Flam from *Reform Judaism* (summer 1994). Copyright © Nancy Flam. Reprinted by permission of Rabbi Nancy Flam.

DEBBIE FRIEDMAN: "Our Power to Touch and Heal" by Debbie Friedman. Reprinted by permission of Debbie Friedman.

HIRSHEL JAFFE, NANCY WECHSLER-AZEN, AND TAMARA GREEN: "Illness is My Teacher" from *Reform Judaism* (summer 1994). Reprinted by permission of Rabbi Hirshel Jaffe, Rabbi Nancy Wechsler-Azen, and Tamara Green.

JEWISH LIGHTS PUBLISHING: "A Prayer for Prayer" by Rabbi Sheldon Zimmerman from *Healing of Soul, Healing of Body: Spiritual Leaders Unfold the Strength and Solace of Psalms,* edited by Rabbi Simkha Y. Weintraub (Woodstock, Vt.: Jewish Lights Publishing, 1994); "Divorce is a true passage . . ." by Rabbi Vicki Hollander and "Prayer after a Miscarriage" by Rabbi Sandy Eisenberg Sasso from *Lifecycles,* vol. 1: *Jewish Women on Life Passages and Personal Milestones,* edited by Rabbi Debra Orenstein (Woodstock, Vt.: Jewish Lights Publishing, 1998). Permission granted by Jewish Lights Publishing, P.O. Box 237, Woodstock, VT 05091.

ALFRED A. KNOPF: Prayers by Naomi Levy from *To Begin Again* (New York: Alfred A. Knopf, 1998). Reprinted by permission of Alfred A. Knopf.

NORMA U. LEVITT: "Portal to Light" by Norma U. Levitt. Reprinted by permission of Norma U. Levitt.

LILITH MAGAZINE: "Mastectomy: Twelve Months after Surgery—A Bathing Ritual for the End of Mourning" by Jerilyn Goodman from *Lilith* (fall 1995). Reprinted by permission of *Lilith* magazine.

NATIONAL CENTER FOR JEWISH HEALING: Excerpts from *When the Body Hurts, the Soul Still Longs to Sing,* edited by Rabbi Nancy Flam (San Francisco: The Jewish Healing Center, 1992); "Blessing and Extending the Light: A Ritual of Healing for the Eight Nights of Hanukkah" by Rabbi Simkha Y. Weintraub; "Babylonian Talmud, *Berakhot* 5b" from *The Outstretched Arm* 2, no. 1 (fall 1998); "A Healing Resource for the Jewish High Holiday Season: Psalm 27" by Rabbi Simkha Y. Weintraub from *The Outstretched Arm;* as well as all other excerpts from *The Outstretched Arm.* Reprinted by permission of the National Center for Jewish Healing.

DEBBIE PERLMAN *z"l:* "Five: A Lullaby for Courage," "Nine: For Complete Healing," "Psalm 28: For the Caregivers," "A Song for Comfort before Surgery," and "Ten: For Healing" by Debbie Perlman from *Flames to Heaven: New Psalms for Healing and Praise.* "The Masks of Purim" by Debbie Perlman from *The National Center for Jewish Healing* 2, no. 3 (fall 2000). "How I Spent My Summer Vacation" and "One Hundred Sixty-Five: In the Sukkah" by Debbie Perlman. Copyright © 1995–2002 by Deborah M. Perlman, www.HealingPsalm.com. Reprinted by permission of Debbie Perlman.

THE RECONSTRUCTIONIST: "The Jewish Healing Tradition in Historical Perspective" by Laura J. Praglin and "Reflections of 'Healing' in Contemporary Liberal Judaism" by Rabbi Richard Hirsh from *The Reconstructionist* (spring 1999). Copyright *The Reconstructionist.* Reprinted by permission of *The Reconstructionist.*

REFORM JUDAISM: "Overcoming our Pain: The Life Lessons of Dr. Bernie S. Siegel" by Aron Hirt-Manheimer from *Reform Judaism* (summer 1996). Reprinted by permission of *Reform Judaism* magazine, published by the Union of American Hebrew Congregations.

FAITH ROGOW: "Healing Ritual for Abused Women" by Faith Rogow. Reprinted by permission of Faith Rogow.

ROBERT SAKS: "A *Yizkor* Meditation in Memory of a Parent Who Was Hurtful" by Rabbi Robert Saks. Reprinted by permission of Rabbi Robert Saks.

SH'MA: A JOURNAL OF JEWISH RESPONSIBILITY: "Healing of Body; Healing of Spirit" by Rabbi Nancy Flam from *Sh'ma: A Journal of Jewish Responsibility* 28 (October 3, 1997): 538, used by permission of the author; "A Perspective on Jewish Healing" by Naomi Mark from *Sh'ma: A Journal of Jewish Responsibility* 28 (October 3, 1997): 538. Reprinted by permission of *Sh'ma: A Journal of Jewish Responsibility.* For more information visit www.shma.com.

STEPHANIE SHORE: "I ask God for health . . ." Author unknown, from *Service of Faith, Hope and Healing,* compiled by Cantor Stephanie Shore. Reprinted by permission of Stephanie Shore.

JULIE SPITZER *z"l*: "The Fabric of Life" by Rabbi Julie Spitzer appeared in *MAMM* (June 1999). Reprinted by permission of Abbe Tiger.

SUNY PRESS: "Healing after a Miscarriage" by Merle Feld. Reprinted by permission from *A Spiritual Life: A Jewish Feminist Journey* by Merle Feld, the State University of New York Press © 1999, State University of New York. All rights reserved.

TEMPLE SHALOM: "My Prayer" by Marty Coleman and "A Patient's Prayer" from *And the Meditations of My Heart,* Temple Shalom of Aberdeen, New Jersey. Reprinted by permission of Temple Shalom.

ELLEN M. UMANSKY AND DIANNE ASHTON: "*Mikvah* Ceremony for Laura" by Laura Levitt and Rabbi Sue Ann Wasserman, used by permission of the authors, and "A Ritual of Loss" by Penina Adelman, from *Four Centuries of Jewish Women's Spirituality* (Boston: Beacon Press, 1992), are used by permission of its editors, Ellen M. Umansky and Dianne Ashton.

SIMKHA Y. WEINTRAUB: Translations of Psalms 20, 27, 38, 86, and 102 by Rabbi Simkha Y. Weintraub. Translations © Rabbi Simkha Y. Weintraub, CSW. Reprinted by permission of Rabbi Simkha Y. Weintraub.

ERIC WEISS: "Passage to Wholeness" by Rabbi Eric Weiss from *Reform Judaism* 26, no. 3 (spring 1988). Reprinted by permission of Rabbi Eric Weiss.

WOMEN OF REFORM JUDAISM: "Hope" by Carol Backman and "Courage" by Anita Moise Rosefield Rosenberg from *Covenant of the*

Editor's Note: Hebrew transliterations from previously published works appear as they did in the source publications.

Introduction

A quarter of a century ago, it would have been unusual to attend a regular Shabbat service and hear the rabbi offer a prayer for healing, inviting the congregation to add the names of those for whom they wish healing. It would have been out of the ordinary for a congregation or a Sisterhood to sponsor a special healing service. The planning of a healing ritual would have been looked upon as something curious or strange. And yet today, prayers for healing, special healing services, and even rituals of healing are part of our everyday Jewish landscape.

Healing is not about magic. When Jews get together for a healing service, or a healing ritual, or to recite a prayer for healing, we do so fully aware that our words and heartfelt thoughts may not have a direct, easily quantifiable effect. Yet we believe in the power of prayer and also in the power of community. Jews have always turned to God for help. Our texts are full of references to God as our Rock, our source of comfort in times of trouble, and our source of strength. In our tradition, the psalms especially have long been used as texts to be read for healing and finding inner strength. While it may be a sign of the times that the prayer for healing, the *Mi Shebeirach,* has become a standard feature of a Shabbat service in many synagogues, the prayer itself is not new, but a traditional manifestation of the human need for God's intervention in our suffering.

מִי שֶׁבֵּרַךְ אֲבוֹתֵינוּ,
אַבְרָהָם, יִצְחָק וְיַעֲקֹב,
וְאִמּוֹתֵינוּ, שָׂרָה, רִבְקָה,
רָחֵל וְלֵאָה, הוּא יְבָרֵךְ
וִירַפֵּא אֶת-הַחוֹלֶה

(חוֹלָה)_____ בֶּן
_____ (בַּת).

O God, who blessed our ancestors, Abraham, Isaac and Jacob; Sarah, Rebekah, Rachel and Leah, send Your blessing to _____.

Have mercy on him/her, and graciously restore his/her health and strength. Grant him/her a *refu-a sheleima,* a complete recovery, along with all others who are stricken.

May healing come speedily, and let us say: Amen.

הַקָּדוֹשׁ בָּרוּךְ הוּא יְמַלֵּא
רַחֲמִים עָלָיו (עָלֶיהָ)
לְהַחֲלִימוֹ (לְהַחֲלִימָהּ)
וּלְרַפֵּאותוֹ (וּלְרַפֵּאותָהּ)
לְהַחֲזִיקוֹ (לְהַחֲזִיקָהּ)
וּלְהַחֲיוֹתוֹ (וּלְהַחֲיוֹתָהּ).
וְיִשְׁלַח לוֹ (לָהּ) בִּמְהֵרָה
רְפוּאָה שְׁלֵמָה, רְפוּאַת
הַנֶּפֶשׁ וּרְפוּאַת הַגּוּף, בְּתוֹךְ שְׁאָר חוֹלֵי
יִשְׂרָאֵל הַשְׁתָּא
בַּעֲגָלָה וּבִזְמַן קָרִיב, וְנֹאמַר: אָמֵן.

Rabbi's Manual, CCAR Press, 1998

The *Mi Shebeirach* asks God not simply for the physical healing of the body, *r'fuat haguf,* but for *r'fuat hanefesh,* a healing of the soul. The *Mi Shebeirach* is not a prayer asking for the impossibility of physical immortality or the ability to drink from the fountain of youth. Rather, in mentioning both kinds of healing, our tradition wisely acknowledges that while a healing of the body may not always be possible, a healing of the soul is still a worthy goal. At the same time, the balance given in the prayer to both kinds of healing reminds us that not all illness is physical, that not all hurts are of the body. There are many ways in which we may feel broken, not quite the whole person we once were. The wish for healing is not a wish to simply go back in time to how things were before the illness, but a wish to put the pieces back together in a new way. Significantly, the prayer asks for completeness, for *sh'leimut.* Even in sickness and in pain, whether physical or emotional, we have the potential to reach a completeness of spirit, a completeness of the soul. In the face of suffering, what a gift it is to be able to recognize what life still has to offer, to be able to face tomorrow with acceptance and gratitude.

This volume is meant to help both individuals and groups. For individuals in need of healing or looking for a reading or a resource to help in the healing of another, there is a great deal here that will be of help. For groups such as Sisterhoods, healing circles, caring committees, and men's groups, there is a large variety of material here that will be of great assistance in planning programs on the subject of Jewish healing, as well as in creating actual healing services or rituals. Just as there is no one generic way to heal, there is no one generic experience from which one needs to heal. Some of the material included in this volume relates to illness, but there is much more as well, including healing from emotional suffering and from traumatic experiences such as mastectomy, rape, abortion, spousal abuse, or the death of a loved one.

Part 1 is a group of essays that help lay the ground for the work of Jewish healing. What is the history of Jewish healing? How does healing fit into the Jewish tradition? How have Jews traditionally approached the subject of healing? Why the change of approach in recent years? How can prayer actually help in healing? This collection helps answer these questions and explore healing in a Jewish context.

Personal writings on Jewish healing are offered in part 2. Here are testimonies and stories by those who have experienced healing first-hand. These moving stories, told from a variety of personalities and perspectives, show the impact of healing on individual lives.

Part 3 includes traditional passages about healing culled from our sacred texts. There are selections from the *Tanach,* including a collection of psalms related to healing compiled and translated by Rabbi Simkha Weintraub of the National Jewish Healing Center. This sampling of sacred texts related to healing gives an idea of traditional Jewish responses to illness and suffering.

Additional inspirational readings from a variety of contemporary sources, including poetry and modern psalms as well as reinterpretations of traditional blessings and prayers, are provided in part 4. Some of these selections, like "A Prayer for Prayer" or "A Prayer for

Strength," address the need for healing and connection with God in general ways. Others, like "A Song for Comfort before Surgery," "On the Loss of a Child," or "A *Yizkor* Meditation in Memory of a Parent Who Was Hurtful," are suited for specific situations. Parts 3 and 4 both provide material for personal prayer and reflection, as well as helpful resources for healing services.

Part 5 offers resources for rituals of healing, ceremonies created for the specific purpose of healing from a particular experience. Included are rituals on healing after mastectomy, rape, miscarriage, and spousal abuse. Also included are rituals for healing from anger, from emotional trauma, and after a medical scare. These rituals are offered both for use in these specific situations and to serve as models for the creation of other rituals to meet needs for healing. What is clear from reading this selection of rituals is that there is no one way to create, structure, and design a healing ritual. A successful ritual is one in which the specific needs and personality of the person in need of healing are taken into account.

Part 6 focuses on holidays and healing. Along with the growth of Jewish healing centers has come a wonderful array of materials related to healing that can be inserted into the cycle of Jewish life. This section includes additions for the Passover Haggadah, readings for the High Holy Days, and material connected to Purim. In their acknowledgment of the need for healing even at times of holiday and celebration, these readings can provide great comfort.

A compendium of additional resources is offered in part 7. With the increased interest in healing in recent years has come an incredibly rich harvest of books and other materials related to healing. In addition to written material, there are other resources within the Jewish world, such as the various Jewish healing centers around the country and programs run by different Jewish organizations. Again, these resources will be of great help for programs and services, as well as individual study.

There is another group of important resources that are not mentioned within the body of this guide, but bear mentioning here. These are the people and the institutions of the Jewish community. The various Jewish healing centers around the country are one obvious place to seek help, support, and resources. Rabbis and cantors can also be invaluable resources, both to help with personal healing and to help create programming related to healing. Speak to them and include them in programmatic planning. Women of Reform Judaism (WRJ), the UAHC Department of Jewish Family Concerns, the Department of Religious Living of the UAHC, the National Federation of Temple Brotherhoods (NFTB), and the Central Conference of American Rabbis (CCAR) are all important resources as well. They can be sources for samples of healing rituals and services, appropriate liturgy and music, and additional resources for personal support and healing.

Work on this volume was begun in the spring of 2001. Little did we know at the time just how much we would all be in need of healing by the time it was ready to go to press. The events of the last two years have made the need for healing become clearer than ever to me. Just as there is no one way of experiencing pain or trauma, there is no one way to heal, and no one way to bring about healing. Healing is not about forgetting, or even necessarily about overcoming, but it is about moving on. It is about gaining the ability to move forward, to reenter life, albeit often in a new and different way, to be able to once again experience joy and to connect with others.

Let us hope that we all find some measure of healing in the days, months, and years to come and that we are able to find comfort and support in the words of our texts and the support of our families, friends, communities, and congregations.

Kein y'hi ratzon—May it be God's will.

Rabbi Hara E. Person

I

ON
JEWISH
HEALING

The Jewish Healing Tradition
in Historical Perspective[1]

LAURA J. PRAGLIN

Judaism's relation to the themes of healing and curing, and to sickness and health, may be found throughout biblical sources and in later textual and folk interpretations of those sources. Ancient Israel's covenantal relationship affirmed God alone as healer, source of both health and illness, and restorer of body and spirit. Sickness, therefore, was viewed as a divinely ordained form of individual or collective punishment, rather than attributed, as in Mesopotamian, Egyptian, and Canaanite cultures, to independent, demonic forces. God's healing, moreover, was linked to individual and communal forgiveness, restoration, renewal, reward, and deliverance from destruction.[2]

The root word rp', the basis of the Hebrew word for healing and healer, was closely related both to spiritual and physical redemption and to wholeness. In Genesis, God heard the plea of Abraham and healed Abimelech; God promised to keep Israel healthy if she kept the commandments (Gen. 20:17; Exod. 15:26; Deut. 32:39). Deuteronomy 24:8–9 and Numbers 12 recall Moses' prayers for Miriam's healing, and in the Song of Moses, God states: "I deal death and give life; I wounded and I will heal: None can deliver from My hand" (Deut. 32:39). Similar statements appear throughout the Hebrew Bible (Exod. 12:12; 1 Sam. 5:6; 2 Chron. 26:20; Job 5:17–18; Pss. 30:2, 41:4, 103:3, 147:30). The prophetic voices in Hosea, Isaiah, and Jeremiah emphasized the healing aspects inherent in turning back to God (Isa. 6:10, 19:22, 30:26; Hos. 6:15; Jer. 3:22, 17:14, 30:17, 33:6). Ezekiel and Zechariah described God as caretaker of the sick, the weak, and the lost, while rebuking Israel for not aiding God with such efforts on behalf of the needy (Ezek. 34:4; Zech. 11:15–17). Elijah, Elisha, and Isaiah invoked God's healing powers through signs, fasting, prayer, and various healing remedies (1 Kings 17:17–24; 2 Kings 2:20–22, 4:19–37, 20; Isa. 38:1–6; 2 Sam. 12:16–23).

Physician, Priest, and Prophet

The Hebrew Bible, in fact, generally possessed a negative attitude toward physicians, given their perceived link to sorcery and incantations. The practice of such magical or faith healing was, moreover, consistently denounced in Exodus, Leviticus, and Deuteronomy. Consulting exorcists in the search for cure constituted grounds for exile from community or death; the use of magic or incantations was considered an "abomination to the Lord" (Exod. 22:18; Lev. 19:26, 31, 20:6, 27; Deut. 18:9–14). Second Chronicles, for example, mocked foreign doctors' treatments as idolatrous. King Asa of Judah "did not seek the Lord, but sought help from physicians," and as punishment, the Chronicler inferred, he soon died (2 Chron. 16:12).[3] Magical healing practices were condemned as well by the prophets and later in the Mishnah.[4] Even in the 19th and 20th centuries, opponents to the Jewish and Christian Science or other faith healing movements have drawn support from such texts.

Since Israelite priests and prophets closely understood the divine connection to health and healing through sacrifice, prayer, repentance, or fasting, they, rather than physicians, were often consulted in cases of illness.[5] Priestly sacrifice and purification rituals were performed, given the perceived link between illness and ritual impurity. Yet, traditional scholarship has maintained that these rites, unlike ancient pagan exorcism practices, were not intended to combat evil powers through spells or incantations. Rather, prayers for the forgiveness of sins were considered effective against disease; psalms of confession and petition were recited only in the first person, rather than by a priest, and ritual purification occurred only after sickness had passed. Thanks and offerings were brought only later by those who were healed through God's will.[6]

Convincing recent scholarship, however, contends that even in biblical times, healing practices involving magical spells, incantations, and exorcisms had found considerable expression. This was especially true in those Jewish communities influenced by Egyptian, Midianite, or Roman culture, as Numbers, Isaiah, 2 Chronicles, Ezekiel, and 2 Kings attest.[7] The book of Numbers documents Moses fashioning an image (later destroyed by King Hezekiah) known to magically heal serpent bites.[8] First Kings, as well as Josephus, depict Solomon as a magician who could repel demons with his incantations, although the Mishnah records Hezekiah's suppression of this "Book of Cures," given its use as a substitute for prayer.[9] The Apocrypha also documented folk medicine practices featuring the angel Raphael, who brought health and healing in the name of God.[10] According to Philo and Josephus, the Essenes were particularly interested in physical and spiritual healing. The community at Qumran embellished the story of Abraham's healing of Abimelech, while the Dead Sea Scrolls record Abraham healing on behalf of the pharaoh by expelling a plague caused by a demon.[11]

Jewish Healing in the Post-Biblical Tradition

Judaism in the post-biblical period witnessed an increase in the use of various healing remedies, including exorcism of demons and the use of amulets.[12] In the century following the destruction of the Second Temple in 70 C.E., Josephus described the rise of prophetic magicians who largely replaced the Temple priests in meeting individual needs for atonement, guidance, and healing.[13] Such magical healing practices, which included exorcism and foretelling the future, reflected not only the decline of the institutionalized priesthood, but also the lack of a systematic practice of medicine and widespread suffering in culture at large. Charismatics—whether magicians, exorcists, witch doctors, healers, or counselors—became increasingly revered, and new groups and institutions were formed around them. Magical healing stories were now widely circulated, featuring special powers of figures such as Elijah or Elisha, or of later rabbis such as Chanina ben Dosa and Yochanan ben Zakkai.[14]

During the codification of the Mishnah, beginning in the third century C.E., the healer posed an inherently dangerous challenge to the emerging institutional and spiritual authority of the priesthood and later developing rabbinical academies. Tales of individual healing magicians were thus downplayed and few healing stories were actually written down.[15] Nevertheless, the genre of the magical healer has survived in the rabbinic literature. The Mishnah mentions the stone of Abraham which cured all who looked at it. It also depicts one sage healing another through prayer and the laying on of hands.[16]

The sages' detailed discussions and frequent denunciations of magic, witchcraft, and sorcery also serve to underscore evidence of widespread popular reliance upon magical healing practices during the period of the codification of the Talmud and Midrash. The Talmud frequently mentions the use of charms for healing, and the rabbis themselves often sanctioned a wide range of magical cures by physicians, including incantations involving God's name and the recitation of biblical passages.[17] The sages even ruled that any practice actually producing a cure was not to be considered superstition.[18]

Such rabbinic rulings resulted from the lack of a clear distinction between science and magic in medical practice in late antiquity, as well as a necessary compromise with popular culture. While some insist that the rabbis themselves were not superstitious or involved in magical cures, it is likely that they as well were not fully exempt from involvement in magical and mystical aspects of the healing arts, despite their official condemnation. It is likely, however, that later rabbis assigned the title of Chasid to some early magicians, in order to include these popular tales in the later canon. They made certain, however, to interject these famous stories with injunctions concerning the importance of prayer and the observance of the law.[19]

As mentioned above, biblical views of the physician were primarily negative, given ancient Israel's concern over the link between healing and idolatry through magic and sorcery. This factor, in addition to halakhic injunctions against uncleanness, which forbade contact with blood and corpses, seriously limited the development and practice of a profession of medicine.[20] True respect for the profession, as well as the specific obligation to heal—so critical to later Jewish views of health—may be traced to the Hellenistic period, where contact with the Stoic concept of natural law and Greek forms of non-magical, "scientific" medicine removed Jewish objections to cures by physicians.[21] The apocryphal book of Ben Sira, in the early second century B.C.E., thus diverged from the attitudes of Exodus or Chronicles, praising the art of medicine and its healers as instruments of God's will.[22] Nevertheless, this new respect did not render physicians all-powerful or independent of divine intercession. Ben Sira, for instance, stressed that God could also be appealed to directly through prayer, sacrifice, and adherence to the commandments.[23]

Jewish Healing in the Rabbinic Tradition

Despite biblical antecedents, the Mishnah, Talmud, and Midrash became normative sources for subsequent Jewish views of health and healing. The Talmud, in fact, prohibited Jews from living in a city without a physician.[24] Yet rabbis also debated whether medicine represented inappropriate human intervention in God's plan. While the *Tanakh* (Hebrew Bible) and subsequent talmudic authors did continue to depict God delivering illness as punishment for sin, the finality of such decrees were also challenged in every age.

The Talmud recorded the rabbinical consensus that God himself authorized—in fact required—medicine and healing, construing Exodus 21:19–20, which stipulated that the victim of injury must be "thoroughly healed," to mean that God had granted the physician permission to cure. They also interpreted the command to restore lost property in Deuteronomy 22:2 to require restoration of another's body as a form of personal property, thus indicating an obligation to assist another person in life-threatening situations.[25] Rabbis also discerned sanctions to heal, and further grants of authority to physicians, in Leviticus 19:18 ("You shall love your neighbor as yourself"), as well as in Leviticus 19:16 ("Nor shall you stand by the blood of your fellow").

The body, the rabbis taught, was created by God, and thus was both good and a source of intricate wonder. Unlike gnosticism or other Greek philosophies, the rabbis did not believe that the body entrapped the soul, nor that it was a primary source of evil or sin.

Legitimate worldly and physical pleasures, such as food and sex, were intended by God to be enjoyed rather than withheld. As a result, they strongly condemned the ascetic and monastic currents in Christianity. While rabbis recognized essential constraints to earthly pleasures, "any assumption of further limits on the part of human beings was an act of both pride and ingratitude."[26] Rabbinic law thus spelled out legal as well as practical obligations to one's body regarding diet, exercise, sexual relations, hygiene, and sleep. Throughout the ages, rabbis also attempted to illuminate the link between ethical and psychological behavior in the cultivation of mental health. The tractate of the Mishnah comprising *Pirkey Avot* (Sayings of the Fathers) focused upon those behaviors and values which fostered a balanced life, ultimately leading to prevention and cure of mental illness.

Rabbinic interpretations, however varied throughout the ages, maintained that mental health was to be treated as seriously as physical health, given the intricate link between human body and soul. B. *Yoma* 82, for instance, decreed that a threat to mental health *(teruf da'at)* was "to be treated like *piku'ach nefesh,* a threat to one's physical life."[27] Both mental and physical illness, therefore, required that rabbi and physician summon all known powers of cure. Definitions and precipitants of insanity and other incapacities became of primary rabbinic and communal concern, for such diagnoses could determine a Jew's obligation to carry out the full range of *mitzvot.* No less than physical illness, rabbis considered mental incapacity a condition requiring efforts at healing and cure, rather than punishment or repentance.[28]

Healing in Codes and Liturgy

From the tenth to the mid-eighteenth centuries, responsa literature and codes, such as Maimonides' *Mishneh Torah* and Joseph Caro's *Shulchan Arukh,* became major sources of decision-making in Jewish communities, particularly in areas where central Jewish authority was fragmented. Rabbis continued to consider the role of folk healing traditions seriously in their rulings, however, often arriving at compromises between them and the newly-formulated codes. Caro's *Shulchan Arukh* explicitly stated that the Torah mandates the physician to heal, and decreed that withholding treatment was akin to shedding blood.[29] The injunction to heal included non-Jews as well, based partly on interpretation of Leviticus 25:35, insisting upon fair treatment of strangers in one's midst, and partly for pragmatic reasons, to encourage good relations with Christian or Arab neighbors. Such rulings permitted Jewish physicians to treat non-Jews, a particular benefit for northern European Christians, who often sought out cures from Jewish doctors, despite church condemnation and subsequent castigation of Jews as either sorcerers or poisonous murderers, depending upon the outcome of the treatment.[30]

The Jewish obligation to heal extended beyond physicians to the Jewish community at large, where all persons were required to visit the sick.[31] This injunction was intended both to help the ill person, and to imitate God's actions as healer; those who refused committed an infraction akin to bloodshed.[32]

Since God had provided and sanctioned humans to heal others, rabbis regarded the divine-human relationship between persons and God in recovery to be complimentary.[33] Yet God remained the sole healer; doctors, visitors, and hospitals could act as partners and agents of God, never substitutes. The rabbis considered God to reside directly above the invalid's pillow,[34] and one was healed only if ultimately it was God's will. As a result, petitionary prayers to heal the sick, acknowledging God as the ultimate physician, came to be recited from the siddur as part of the traditional liturgy three times per day. The *Amidah* allowed for the insertion of specific petitions for restoring health.[35] So too did *Mi Sheberakh* prayers—recited during the reading of the Torah on the Sabbath—which petitioned God to send "a healing of soul and a healing of body" to ill persons not present.[36] In this vein, European Jews of the sixteenth through eighteenth centuries compiled extensive prayer manuals for healing the sick, which included elements of petition, confession, and gematria.[37] They also developed extensive community curing rituals, formed brotherhoods to visit the sick, established inns for the infirm, and encouraged the founding of Jewish hospitals in many European cities.

Folk Traditions

Other than prayer and visiting the sick, the Talmud repeatedly cautioned against cures involving heretical books, idolatrous foods, or immoral actions.[38] Nevertheless, Jewish mystics continued to practice numerous folk healing traditions until the modern period. This was especially true when authoritative texts failed to address particular situations, allowing popular practices to supplant or even contradict rabbinical sanctions. Torah scrolls were at times placed on sick bodies to encourage healing, while *Kiddush* wine was applied to the eyes.[39] Astrology and amulets were also widely used well into the sixteenth century. Rabbi Solomon Luria, in fact, even condoned consulting non-Jewish magicians for cures for illnesses caused by magic or evil spirits.[40]

While the Talmud prescribed a variety of specific medical remedies, some rabbis decreed that certain of these cures, including talmudic exorcisms, were anachronistic, potentially dangerous, and could possibly expose rabbis to ridicule. In lieu of talmudic therapies, Jewish physicians employed accepted contemporary medical practices, reasoning "that the religious imperative was to cure and that the Talmudic prescriptions were simply suggestions based upon the medicine of that time."[41] In addition to prayer, medieval commentators such as Rashi and Maimonides suggested the close connection between health and obedience to God through following the commandments. For the rabbi-physician Maimonides, one was obliged to care for the body since the soul's well-being depended on it. He viewed sickness less as a divine judgment than as an opportunity to exercise human powers of cure. Nevertheless, one had to be physically healthy to follow God's commandments, for it was "impossible during sickness to have any understanding or knowledge of the Creator."[42]

Advocating Aristotle's golden mean in balancing personality characteristics, Maimonides also wrote extensively about insanity and its link to legal and moral responsibility, since those deemed insane were exempt from the expectations of halakhic observance. Nachmanides, too, worked to aid individuals deemed insane, in order to restore their halakhic status. In fact, wrote Nachmanides, saving a person's soul or mental health was placed in the category of *piku'ach nefesh,* or the saving of one's life, thus permitting the waiver of nearly all obligations in pursuit of such restoration of health.[43]

Jewish Healing in the Chasidic Tradition

The Jewish Chasidic tradition, emerging in the seventeenth and eighteenth centuries, brought with it intense interest in the role of sin, illness, magic, and spiritual and physical healing.[44] The founder of the Chasidic movement, Israel ben Eliezer, also known as the Ba'al Shem Tov, often suggested healing methods at odds with those of Jewish physicians. Chasidism generally maintained the link between sin and disease, viewing divine punishment to result from one's failure to follow the commandments. Physical and mental healing thus involved reestablishing a right relationship with God through such acts as prayer, devotional reading of psalms, fasting, and secret acts of charity. The *tzadikim* of the later Chasidic tradition were also considered great healing practitioners. Some relied upon the curing remedies of the Ba'al Shem Tov, while others focused primarily on prayer. Rabbi Nachman of Bratzlav was unusual, however, in banning the intervention of doctors and relying solely on prayer.[45]

In addition to Chasidism, other developments enriched the connection between Judaism and mental healing. Musar, a nineteenth century European-Russian Jewish movement stressing ethics and self-scrutiny, witnessed a proliferation of ethical-psychological texts which promoted the cultivation of certain behaviors and values in the quest for a balanced life. Such a balance, the proponents believed, could prevent and/or even cure mental illness.[46]

Jewish Healing in the Modern Period

Massive changes in Jewish identity and self-perception followed the European Enlightenment and subsequent "emancipation" from ghetto life. Beginning in the late eighteenth century, many Jews adopted an ethic of Western liberal individualism over against more traditional and communal-oriented forms of meaning, belonging, knowing, and understanding.[47] The dilemma for these Jews, once the initial excitement of liberalization and religious reform waned, was that they found themselves denuded of the psychic richness, spontaneity, and close-knit character of traditional Judaism, but were unable to go back to it, or to recapture these emotional components in the newer religious forms. By the late nineteenth century, most Western Jews were no longer immune to the prevailing modern sense of rootlessness and anomie.

In an attempt to address the widespread psychic hunger of congregants for meaning and spiritual healing, some rabbis and congregants in the early twentieth century began to look to the new discipline of psychology, with its concern with mental healing and the inner self. Given its "scientific" claims,[48] it was embraced eagerly by rabbinic counselors to gain respectability for their enterprise. Yet psychology also encouraged rabbis to redefine the relationship of Judaism to medicine and mental healing, to examine classic roles of the rabbi as priest, and to define concepts of human nature and the soul. Such examination helped to clarify and reformulate little-known or forgotten aspects of the Jewish healing tradition and enabled revitalization of Jewish spiritual and affective life largely lost in the wake of secularization and modernization.

Rabbinic reactions to psychology varied widely, depending upon historical contexts and social locations. Rabbis were able to appreciate Freud, for instance, only by reaching beyond the initial affront of Freud's cultural critique of religion as obsessional neurosis, to an appreciation of his revolutionary clinical understandings of unconscious motivations, psychic development, and the dynamics of psychopathology. Moreover, those rabbis who welcomed psychology as a way to recapture the roles of counselor and spiritual guide stressed that Judaism *did* possess such precedents for healing and pastoral care in scriptural, rabbinic, and later Chasidic literature, although liberal Judaism had been cut off from such precedents.

In traditional circles, however, there remained the concern that rabbis not involve themselves in therapeutic issues that might pit the individual against religious tradition and the community. Instead, rabbis should provide solace and advice at life-cycle events, focusing their counsel upon the individual's soul and conscience, but with the consistent aim of atonement and reintegration into the community. They pointed to the well-developed body of Jewish literature, to which a rabbi need only to turn and apply, that spelled out the distinct roles of the rabbi as well as definitions of physical, moral, and spiritual health and illness. Why, then, turn to psychology for answers when the Jewish tradition had provided such guidance for hundreds of generations?

Drawing on the Past for the Present

The contemporary interest in Judaism and healing builds on a long history of prior experience and analysis. As Jewish tradition has evolved and adapted to accommodate to new settings and developments, opinions, rituals, and theologies relating to healing have also evolved and changed. The resources and citations and texts of tradition provide an important starting point for the contemporary conversation. Where this conversation will take us, and how contemporary Judaism will respond to the current interest in healing, will depend, in part, on how we use the resources of the past to meet the needs of the present.

Notes

1. This article is an abbreviated version of Chapter I of my University of Chicago dissertation entitled "The Rabbinate After Freud: American Rabbinical Responses to Psychological Thought and Practice, 1912–1980" (Ann Arbor: UMI Dissertation Services [no. 9823019], 1998).

2. Howard Clark Kee, "Medicine and Healing," in *Anchor Bible Dictionary* (New York: Doubleday, 1992), 659.

3. See also Jer. 8:22–9:6, 46:11, 51:8; Hos. 5:13; Job 13:4.

4. Isa. 3:2–3; Ezek. 13:17–20; Jer. 27:9–10; M. *Sanhedrin* 7:11; B. *Sanhedrin* 68a.

5. Madeline S. Miller and J. Lane Miller, "Medicine in Israel," in *Harper's Encyclopedia of Bible Life* (New York: Harper & Row, 1978), 69. On healing precedents in ancient Judaism, see Elliot N. Dorff, "The Jewish Tradition," in *Caring and Curing: Health and Medicine in the Western Religious Traditions*, ed. Ronald L. Numbers and Darrel W. Amundsen (New York: Macmillan, 1986), 5–39; and David M. Feldman, *Health and Medicine in the Jewish Tradition* (New York: Crossroad, 1986).

6. Yehezkel Kaufmann, *The Religion of Israel: From Its Beginnings to the Babylonian*

Exile, trans. Moshe Greenberg (New York: Schocken, 1960), 107–9; Jacob Milgrom, *Leviticus 1–16: A New Translation with Introduction and Commentary* (New York: Doubleday, 1991), 23–33.

7. Isa. 3:2–3; 2 Chron. 33:6; Ezek. 13:18–20; 2 Kings 4:22–37. See Emil Schürer, *The Literature of the Jewish People in the Time of Jesus*, ed. Nahum N. Glatzer (New York: Schocken, 1972), 151–5; and I. Tzvi Abusch, "Physicians," in *Harper's Bible Dictionary* (New York: Harper & Row, 1985), 796.

8. Num. 21:8–9; 2 Kings 18:4.

9. 1 Kings 12, 13; M. *Pesakhim* 4:9.

10. Tobit 3:16.

11. Philo, *De Vita Contemplativa* 2; Josephus, *Jewish War*, 2:136; *Genesis Apocryphon* (1QapGen) 20:12–29.

12. Kaufmann, 109.

13. John Dominic Crossan, *The Historical Jesus: The Life of a Mediterranean Jewish Peasant* (San Francisco: Harper Collins, 1991), 137–67.

14. B. *Berakhot* 34a.

15. Crossan, 137–67.

16. B. *Bava Batra* 16b; B. *Berakhot* 5b.

17. B. *Shabbat* 67a; B. *Gitin* 69a.

18. M. *Shabbat* 6:10; B. *Eruvin* 67a.

19. John P. Meier, *A Marginal Jew: Rethinking the Historical Jesus*, Anchor Bible Reference Library, Volume 2 (New York: Doubleday, 1994), 581.

20. Miller and Miller, 69.

21. Dorff, 22; Kee, 661; see also Fred Rosner, *Medicine in the Bible and the Talmud* (New York: KTAV, 1977).

22. Sirach 38:1–12.

23. Rebecca T. Alpert, "From Jewish Science to Rabbinical Counseling: The Evaluation of the Relationship between Religion and Health by the American Reform Rabbinate, 1916–1954" (Dissertation, Temple University, 1978), 34.

24. B. *Sanhedrin* 17b.

25. B. *Bava Kama* 85a; B. *Sanhedrin* 73a.

26. Dorff, 9.

27. Feldman, 49.

28. Dorff, 25.

29. Dorff, 16; *Shulchan Arukh*, Yoreh De'ah 336:1.

30. Dorff, 17.

31. *Shulchan Arukh*, Yoreh De'ah 335:2.

32. B. *Sotah* 14a; B. *Nedarim* 40a; Maimonides, *Mishneh Torah*, Laws of Mourning 14:4.

33. *Leviticus Rabbah* 16.8.

34. B. *Shabbat* 12b.

35. Joseph Hertz, ed., *Authorized Daily Prayer Book* (New York: Bloch, 1948), 134.

36. Hertz, 492.

37. Jacob R. Marcus, *Communal Sick-Care in the German Ghetto* (Cincinnati: HUC Press, 1947), 22–24.

38. *Shemot Rabbah* 16; M. *Sanhedrin* 10:1.

39. Joshua Trachtenberg, *Jewish Magic and Superstition: A Study in Folk Religion* (Cleveland: World, 1961), 144.

40. Solomon Luria, *Responsa* (Furth, 1768), quoted in Dorff, 22.

41. *Tosafot*, Mo'ed Katan 11a; Jacob ben Moses Mollin, *Yalkutai Maharil*; Joseph Caro, Kesef Mishneh commentary to *Mishneh Torah*, Laws of Ethics 4:18; Gombiner, *Magen*

Avraham commentary to *Shulchan Arukh,* Orakh Chayim 173, quoted in Dorff, 21, 37.

42. Maimonides, *Mishneh Torah,* Hilchot Deot: 4.

43. *The Writings of Nachmanides,* trans. Charles B. Chavel, Volume 2 (New York: Shilo, 1978), 43.

44. See Gershom Scholem, *Shabbatai Zevi: Mystical Messiah,* trans. R.J. Zwi Werblowsky (Princeton: Princeton University Press, 1973), 626.

45. Simon Dubnow, *Toledot HaHasidut* (Tel Aviv: Dvir, 1967), 300.

46. Arnold Rachlis, "The Musar Movement and Psychotherapy," *Judaism* 23 (Summer 1974): 337; Zalman Ury, *The Musar Movement* (New York: Yeshiva University Press, 1970); and Menachem Glenn, *Israel Salanter* (New York: Bloch, 1943).

47. Emil Durkheim, *Suicide: A Study in Sociology,* trans. John A. Spaulding and George Simpson (Glencoe, IL: Free Press, 1951), 252–53. See also John Murray Cuddihy, *The Ordeal of Civility: Freud, Marx, Levi-Strauss, and the Jewish Struggle with Modernity* (Boston: Beacon, 1974), 10.

48. Philip Rieff, *The Triumph of the Therapeutic: Uses of Faith After Freud* (New York: Harper, 1966); Peter Berger, "Towards a Sociological Understanding of Psychoanalyis," *Social Research* 32 (1965): 26–41.

The Jewish Way of Healing*

RABBI NANCY FLAM

When Eve W. was diagnosed with lymphoma, she sought the finest medical treatment available. But she wanted more than high-tech medicine could offer. Like millions of Americans, she supplemented her medical treatment with complementary therapy. Eve began to practice Buddhist meditation, Hindu yoga, and natural diet. Deeply committed to her Judaism, Eve was nonetheless unaware of Jewish practices for strengthening the body and spirit at times of illness.

In response to his AIDS diagnosis, David M. began seeing one specialist after another. In addition, he tried to meet his emotional challenges by working with a therapist, taking part in a 12-step group, and staying in contact with close friends. Then, one day he saw an advertisement for a "Spiritual Support Group for HIV+ Jews." With no clear sense of what he might gain, he called the number and registered for the group.

Shoshanna A. had never been religious or Jewishly affiliated. But when she was diagnosed with metastatic breast cancer, she called the Jewish Healing Center. "I rebelled against Judaism all my life. I couldn't deal with the sexism of my brothers getting Jewish educations and fancy bar mitzvahs while I got nothing. So social activism became my religion. But now I'm sick and I'm not sure how to cope, and I wonder what I've been rejecting all these years. Maybe Judaism has something to offer me?"

Eve, David, and Shoshanna's cases are typical. In times of sickness, pain, and trouble, many Jews seek spiritual comfort and healing

---

*The ideas for this essay were formulated with Rabbi Amy Eilberg.

through non-Jewish means, such as twelve-step recovery programs, new-age communities, and mind-body institutions. For some, however, there may come a point when one turns toward the Jewish tradition and community to see what it has to offer. Such seekers can find abundant resources in Judaism, which has addressed questions of health and recovery for millennia.

Body and Spirit

Jewish tradition has long recognized that there are two components of health: the body and the spirit. The *Mi Sheberach* prayer, traditionally recited for someone who is ill, asks God for *refuah shleima*, a complete healing, and then specifies two aspects: *refuat hanefesh*, healing of the soul/spirit/whole person, and *refuat haguf*, cure of the body. To cure the body means to wipe out the tumor, clear up the infection, or regain mobility. To heal the spirit involves creating a pathway to sensing wholeness, depth, mystery, purpose, and peace. Cure may occur without healing, and healing without cure. Pastoral caregivers and family members of seriously ill people know that sometimes lives and relationships are healed even when there is no possibility of physical cure; in fact, serious illness often motivates people to seek healing of the spirit.

Recent research in the mind-body field suggests that the disease process itself may be affected by psychosocial healing; mind and spirit may not be as separate from the biochemistry of physical illness as we once thought. For instance, Dr. David Spiegel of Stanford University found that women with metastatic breast cancer who participated in a one-year support group lived significantly longer than women who received similar medical treatment without a support group (*Healing and the Mind*, Doubleday). Being part of a meaningful community that encourages self-expression can affect the course of an illness.

At the point when Shoshanna turned toward the Jewish community, she was not expecting to find a physical cure, but she desperately hoped for healing of the spirit. Shoshanna needed to overcome her negative association with Judaism in order to benefit from its religious wisdom. With great hunger for spiritual nourishment, she enrolled in a seminar about Jewish views of health and illness, took part in a study group exploring Judaism and feminism, and began attending regular "Services of Healing," where Jews dealing with illness and grief pray together for strength and comfort. At 50 years of age, she began her own journey of Jewish learning and spiritual development.

Spiritual Healing: *Bikur Cholim*

A fundamental feature of Jewish spiritual healing is *bikur cholim* (visiting the sick), which responds to two of the greatest burdens of contemporary life: isolation and lack of community. At a time of illness, *bikur cholim* offers us the comfort of human connection and interdependence, a sense of community we so desperately need.

The mitzvah of *bikur cholim* helps fulfill the obligation to "love our neighbor as ourself," and it is required of every Jew (Maimonides, *Mishneh Torah: Laws of Mourning*, ch. 14). Like comforting mourners and performing other acts of kindness, *bikur cholim* brings goodness to the world (*Avot de Rabbi Natan* 39:1).

By participating in the spiritual support group for HIV+ Jews, David had his first positive adult experience of Jewish community. Having been rejected by the Jewish community during his adolescence because of being gay, David had, in turn, rejected Judaism. It was only later, in his mid-40s, emboldened by a sense that he now had "nothing to lose," that David met with other Jews for support and comfort. His experience in the spiritual support group radically changed his attitude toward Judaism, as he grew to see that in fact there was a place for him. Having looked to eastern religions for a spiritual home in his young adulthood, David was relieved to find that he "no longer had to knock on any doors; the door to tradition was open." When the group came to a close, David and two other participants joined a local Reform synagogue. The ensuing *bikur cholim* visits provided by synagogue members and Jewish professionals bolstered him tremendously during the difficult days of illness that lay ahead.

A visitor's attentive presence breaks the isolation and sense of abandonment, the existential aloneness often felt by one who is sick, reaffirming the person's essential humanness and wholeness. In addition, the visitor provides a link to community, reaffirming a sense of connection and purpose.

Torah teaches that one who practices *bikur cholim* imitates God, whose presence visited Abraham after his circumcision (Genesis Rabbah 8:13). The sources teach that each of us is visited by God's presence when we are ill, which we may interpret as feeling a sense of hope, care, and protection. This is exactly what a loving visitor can inspire. The Codes teach that God's presence rests upon the head of the bed of anyone who is sick, and that we must not sit there for fear of blocking it (Maimonides, *Mishneh Torah: Laws of Mourning,* ch. 14). This suggests that the visitor must reflect and not obscure God's presence when attending to the person who is ill.

Bikur cholim demonstrates the healing power of relationship. There are many stories in the Talmud about Rabbi Yohanan ben Zakkai, famed for his power to heal. When he heard of another rabbi who was sick, he would visit and speak with him about his suffering. After speaking, Yohanan ben Zakkai would hold out his hand, and the other rabbi would rise. One day Yohanan ben Zakkai fell ill. He was visited by Rabbi Hanina, who, after speaking to the stricken sage, held out his hand, and Yohanan ben Zakkai stood up. "Why couldn't Yohanan ben Zakkai raise himself?" the disciples asked, as he was known to be a great healer. The answer: "Because the prisoner cannot free himself from prison" (Berachot 5b). Here we learn that even the greatest of Jewish healers needed another person to help free himself from the prison of fear, hopelessness, and isolation.

Spiritual Healing: Prayer

In addition to *bikur cholim,* Jewish tradition teaches that we should pray for ourselves and others during a time of illness. Many modern Jews are resistant to praying in general, and especially skeptical about praying for something specific, such as good health or a cure.

One reason such prayer can be difficult is that we may not envision God in a classically Jewish way, as One who hears prayers and answers or fails to answer them. Another reason is that we often feel unjustly afflicted; when we have led ethical lives but nonetheless find ourselves struggling with disease, we may feel that God has been unfair. Instead of rejecting God, however, we might instead reject some aspects of classical Jewish theology (such as the idea that God rewards good with good), and search for a more satisfying way to think about God's ways.

Prayer allows us quiet time for reflection. Like meditation, it can be calming and relaxing, thereby allowing us access to regions of our inner selves. It can help us get in touch with our strength and faith. Prayer can also provide release and relief from anxious thoughts that exacerbate both physical and psychic pain. The mental relaxation of prayer can bring us comfort when we take the perspective that our lives are ultimately in God's hands.

In addition, when we pray in community and use traditional Jewish liturgy, we not only benefit from the company of other Jews, we find comfort in knowing that the words of the psalms and blessings have been spoken by millions of Jews past and present who, like us, yearn for healing.

Before Eve went into the hospital for surgery, she called me for counseling and support. Because she lived far away, I provided support by phone. At the end of our conversation, I asked her if she wanted to pray together. "That would be wonderful," she said. After a moment of centering silence, I offered the *Mi Sheberach* prayer for her. When we were done, she told me that both her doctors were Jewish and asked if I would send them a copy of the *Mi Sheberach*. After her surgery, Eve called to tell me that the operation had gone well. Immediately following the surgery, the doctors had buzzed the administrator from the operating room and requested that she bring in a copy of the *Mi Sheberach*. Eve's two doctors then prayed on her behalf. When her husband described this final ritual of the operating room to Eve after she woke from surgery, she was deeply moved and grateful.

Jewish Tools

The Torah can be a source of healing for the spirit and pysche. Some rabbis "prescribe" sacred verses for use in meditation. For someone who is anxious about her self-worth, a rabbi may recommend she sit quietly, breathe slowly, and for five minutes twice a day repeat this verse: "*Yismach Moshe b'matnat chelko;* Moses was satisfied with his portion." Or for fear, the last lines of "Adon Olam," "*B'yado afkid ruchi, b'eit ishan, v'aira, v'im ruchi geviyati, Adonai li v'lo ira;* Into God's hands I entrust my spirit, when I sleep and when I wake; and with my spirit and my body also, God is with me, I will not fear." Or for insecurity: "*Adonai karov l'chol korav, l'chol asher yikraoohoo ve'emet;* God is near to all who cry out to God, to all who cry out to God in truth." Or to enhance a sense of gratitude: "*Zeh ha'yom asah Adonai, nagila v'nismecha vo;* This is the day that God has made; let us rejoice and be glad in it."

Rabbi Richard Levy of Los Angeles teaches the wisdom of writing the verse and affixing it where one will see it throughout the day: above one's desk, on the telephone key pad, on the dashboard. Meditation upon a verse of Torah, upon the Shema, or upon Hebrew letters can calm the spirit, and bring it into communion with the Divine.

The chasidim have historically made great use of the niggun, the wordless tune, which has become part of many Reform services. By repeating a wordless tune over and over again, or one with nonsense syllables (like "Yai bai bai"), one can begin to still the mind and open the heart. Nonsense syllables are especially helpful, occupying the linear language-making part of our brains so that it is easier to let go of thoughts as they arise. The nonsense syllables function as a mantra whose message is that our being is greater than our thinking.

The psalms have been our primary devotional literature of healing. The rabbis have prescribed different lists of 10, 18, and 36 psalms to be recited at times of illness. These sacred verses invite the person reading them to identify with the psalmist in his pain and longing. Psalms of healing take the reader through a cycle of bewilderment, anguish, complaint, and renewed hope and faith.

Jewish tradition also offers active modes of spiritual healing. When the experience of illness compromises our sense of power, we need to feel that we are contributing to the good of the world by acts of *tzedakah* and *gemilut chassadim* (kindness). For the Jew, *tikun olam* (repair of the world) and *tikun hanefesh* (repair of the soul) are inseparable.

Taking part in Jewish communal life breaks the isolation that often accompanies illness. The mandate *"al tifrosh min hatzibur,* do not separate yourself from the community," is never more important than at a time of illness. Of course, this means that Jewish institutions must be especially responsive to the particular needs of Jews who are ill.

Finally, any amount of personal observance that contributes to feeling that one lives in a meaningful universe is beneficial. Immersion in Jewish ritual, such as the celebration of Shabbat, holiday observance, or Torah study can help heal the spirit, highlighting community, connection, meaning, and God.

Eve, David, and Shoshanna are testimony to Judaism's richness and importance in helping bolster the spirit. Eve recovered beautifully, and now volunteers as a lay counselor with others who are struggling with cancer. Prior to David's death earlier this year, he expressed enormous gratitude for the connection and warmth he felt from the Jewish community. Shoshanna continues to participate in healing services, has joined a synagogue, and participates in a women's Torah study group. In preparing for her own passing, she is guided by the wisdom of Jewish tradition. In a recent conversation, Shoshanna expressed her regret for not having actively brought up her children as Jews, adding: "I think it's not such a bad lesson to leave them with, after all, to see that their mother found her own authentic way to Judaism in her 50s. Maybe they'll follow my example and find their own authentic Jewish paths as well."

Reflections on "Healing"
in Contemporary Liberal Judaism*

RABBI RICHARD HIRSH

. . . so Elisha came into the house, and there was the boy, laid out dead on the couch. He went in, shut the door behind the two of them, and prayed to God. Then he came near the child and placed himself over him. He placed his mouth on the boy's mouth; his eyes on the boy's eyes; his hands on the boy's hands; and the body of the child became warm. Elisha stepped down, walked once up and down the room, then again placed himself over the child. Thereupon the child sneezed seven times, and his eyes opened . . . . (II Kings Chapter 4)

When we speak of "healing," few of us have in mind the sort of physical cure represented in this resurrection myth from the life of the prophet Elisha. We associate such miraculous healing with fundamentalist religion, which advances the assumption that faith alone, especially when mediated through the personality of a charismatic spiritualist, can effect recovery. We cringe at the commercialism and shamelessness of those who hawk healing on late-night cable television, precisely because we recognize the legitimacy of the need and the transparency of the "cure."

---

*The author wishes to express his appreciation to Rabbi Simkha Weintraub, who brought a number of the traditional texts cited in this article to my attention during a teaching session he led at a convention of the Reconstructionist Rabbinical Association.

Rejecting Fundamentalism, Not Healing

However, progressive religious communities should not allow fundamentalist ones to claim ownership of healing, an important dimension of faith, any more than we cede the category of "religion" itself. We need to define and respond to the issues of healing from a liberal Jewish perspective. There are rich spiritual resources in Judaism that respond to the need of healing body and/or soul. A progressive Jewish approach to healing can help provide those tools, in a sensitive and meaningful way that avoids magic and evades a simple supernaturalism.

Healing is not only a vital concern—it is a significant entry point into the Jewish community for many Jews struggling with the relevance of Jewish spiritual tradition to their daily lives. Our concern for those Jews requires us to think through the personal, communal, and theological implications of what liberal Jews mean by healing. We must be able to say what healing means from the perspective of our interpretation of Jewish tradition. We are obligated to be clear to those within our communities about what Judaism can, and cannot, offer in the way of healing.

Towards a Definition of Healing

Healing has become an important and nearly universal issue within progressive Jewish communities. Yet healing risks the fate of "spirituality"—a meaningful term too often employed to refer to such a wide range of experience as to be empty of any compelling or convincing content. A liberal Jewish theology of healing ought to begin with a common understanding of the term.

What do we mean by healing? Following the inclinations of Maimonides, we might begin with what healing is *not* in a liberal Jewish theology. Healing is not necessarily the same as being cured. The type of miraculous recovery presided over (literally!) by Elisha is not to be expected, certainly not what ought to be promised, explicitly or implicitly, as an outcome of Jewish healing.

To the incurably ill who seek healing, the wish-fulfillment possibilities of being cured must surely be tempting. A liberal Jewish theology of healing, however, must not become a partner in the creation of false hope. We must incorporate the tools of the spirit that speak to the *non-rational* dimension of life, while avoiding the magic and superstition that support the *irrational* inclinations that so understandably surface around illness.

Of equal concern: the rabbi who participates in the perpetuation of unrealistic expectations invites upon him/herself the appropriate scorn from the congregant who has entrusted his/her spiritual plight to the community of which the rabbi is a part. Rabbi Alan Bregman, speaking at a meeting of Chicago-area Reform rabbis, recently warned us that without careful monitoring as well as adequate self-consciousness, the "rabbi as healer" invites the narcissistic indulgences of both congregant and rabbi in an age of diminishing rabbinic authority.

Neither Cure nor Recovery

If healing is not necessarily curing, it is also not necessarily recovery. While cure and recovery are near neighbors on the spectrum of healing, they are not identical. The various twelve-step programs share an awareness that cure is ephemeral. One is and remains recovering, rather than recovered.

Jewish healing cannot hold out the promise of recovery any more than it should extend the expectation of cure. Jewish healing services, a newly-emerging liturgical form, should avoid fostering dependency on the part of the weakest. One of our colleagues speaks of a congregant who can no longer pass him in the synagogue hallway without requesting a "blessing," apparently convinced that what stands between her and illness is the divine intervention of "the holy man."

As healing is neither necessarily cure nor recovery in a liberal Jewish theology, it is also not (only) communal and emotional support, as indispensable (and halakhically mandated under the laws of *bikur cholim*) as these may be. Certainly mutual, congregational, and rabbinic support are important, but they cannot by themselves replace the difficult and rewarding personal work of healing in a Jewish context.

When we sponsor a Jewish healing service we hope to create a context for those who share a similar sense of needing resources and renewal. That very togetherness (like the traditional practice of only having mourners rise for *Kaddish*) helps substitute solidarity for solitude. While some may pursue healing as a private path, the communal nature of Judaism suggests that a first step (necessary but not sufficient) is to create a communal context in which the complex emotions of illness and healing can be (discretely and appropriately) shared.

If healing becomes only caring support, however, the efficacy of healing services is likely to become diminished. We need a model of healing in which the congregation and the congregant share expectations as to the path to healing and the challenging *personal* spiritual work that this requires—and which the *community* supports.

One Possible Definition

From a liberal Jewish perspective, then, healing is not limited to, or necessarily correlated with, cure, recovery, or caring. Yet we still need to offer some tentative definition in order to create and provide appropriate words, music, prayer and, perhaps most importantly, theology—God-talk that informs and inspires us on the path to healing.

A liberal Jewish theology of healing might then be based upon the following understanding: *Healing might be understood as the transcendence of illness, of body and/or spirit, through the affirmative response to the blessing of life and the acknowledgment of the gift of living.* This is not only cure, not only recovery, not only caring; it is healing as the worked-for and worked-through path from despair to affirmation, and from denial to acceptance.

Towards a Liberal Jewish Theology of Healing

What are the metaphors and sacred myths about God that support our efforts to make Judaism a resource in the human struggle to overcome brokenness and affirm a transcending wholeness? Who and what is God, and how does God relate to the emerging vocabulary of healing and the rituals of recovery?

Within the 4,000 year old traditions of Judaism, ancient as well as contemporary, there exists a wide range of thinking about God. Many of the dimensions of Jewish theology, from the rational to the mystical, from the personal to the abstract, can be helpful tools in constructing a theology of healing. A truly liberal Judaism—one which is fully pluralistic—should not rule out any resource from within our tradition, but should rather make available the widest possible range of options.

Rather than engage in debate as to whether God is a personal being or a cosmic force, male or female, imminent or transcendent, we can find common ground and move to a common goal by focusing on the attributes of God affirmed in the sacred myths of Judaism. For purposes of constructing a liberal Jewish theology of healing, three of these attributes emerge as essential: God as Creator, God as Revealer, and God as Redeemer.

Three Perspectives

These three attributes, of course, form the triangular foundation of Jewish liturgy and Jewish theology. The morning and evening prayers progress through this sacred cycle with the comforting rhythms of repetition. Jewish prayer begins with reflections on creation/nature *(Ma'ariv Aravim, Yotzer Or)*, moves on to revelation/Torah *(Ahavat Olam/Ahavah Rabbah)* and ascends to redemption/Exodus *(Emet Ve'emunah/Emet Veyatziv)*. Using the corollary attributes of God provides a convenient, traditional, and sacred language for understanding what God may mean for us through the prism of healing.

There is an additional advantage to employing the sacred myths of God as Creator, Revealer, and Redeemer in the enterprise of creating a liberal theology of healing. The traditional prayer for healing, the *Mi Sheberakh* ("May God Who Blessed . . .") speaks of healing in three dimensions: *refu'at haguf*, healing of body; *refu'at hanefesh*, healing of spirit/soul; and *refu'ah shelemah*, a healing of wholeness.

The construction of a liberal theology of healing can begin with the association of each of these dimensions of healing with one of the three sacred attributes of God. Thus: for the healing of body we need a theology of God as Creator; for the healing of spirit/soul, we need a theology of God as Revealer; and for a healing of wholeness, we need a theology of God as Redeemer.

God As Creator—Healing of Body

Many of the illnesses with which we deal are of the body: diseases, chronic conditions, infirmities. In some cases these are treatable, with the treatments varying from those easily administered and endured to those that are painful and problematic in themselves. Put simply, often that for which we seek healing is the very real physical malady that makes our bodily existence uncomfortable, perhaps even unbearable.

Both illness and treatment serve to remind us of the irreducible reality of our physical bodies. Bodily illness forces us to confront the universal circumstance of being: we came into the world at a specific point in time and however reluctantly we accept or admit it, we leave this world at a specific time as well. Our bodies cannot endure eternally.

A liberal Jewish response to the healing needs of the body might begin with a rediscovery of the centrality of creation. We need to focus on the possible meaning implied in the question "why something and not nothing?" Why is there a creation, a physical world, within which each of us lives in a created, physical body? What meaning can we derive from the reality of existence itself?

Tradition and Experience

The answers to these questions arise from two areas: tradition and experience. As Jews, we affirm the Torah tradition that existence itself is the creation of God; without God, there is no world. Since God did not have to create the world, the act of creation itself is a gift of the Creator. The life we live within that creation can become a gift as well.

From experience we know, even in our most bitter moments of affliction, that life has also yielded moments of joy, love, and wonderment, many of which are directly dependent on our created bodies. A hug from a grandchild in which the grandparent feels, quite literally, the reality of generativity, is different from the reassurance conveyed by an "I love you" uttered over a long-distance phone call. The sensual solidarity conveyed in the intimacy of sexual relations provides a physical complement to the emotional affirmations shared by loving partners.

Healing of body begins when we refuse to allow current or chronic physical affliction to rob us of the reality of the pleasure and meaning that our body has allowed us to enjoy. It is the reclaiming of our body from the ravages of illness.

Healing of body may begin with a simple touch, with an affirmation of body and by implication of the soul within that body, each part being united in the "divine image" in which all are created. The simple gesture of holding a hand becomes an endorsement of dignity. Healing of body is supported by the comfort of contact.

Creation and the Body

A liberal Jewish healing service ought to include prayer, song, and study that renews and supports our faith in God as Creator, as the One who calls life into being and confers *kavod* (honor, dignity, respect) on those created ones within the world. As those who are ill often correctly remind us, they are people who happen to have an illness; they are not the illness itself.

This insight, by the way, ought to encourage us to examine the relative benefits and potential losses inherent in the creation of separate "healing services." An alternative is incorporating a prayer/moment of healing within *existing* services. What is the balance of individual/community and healthy/ill when we create a service devoted entirely to healing? What is the message about who people are in their totality?

Awareness of creation and of our bodies as part of creation also enables us to accept with less fear the inevitable end of each life. In Judaism, God alone is Creator, and the creation in which we live, while God's gift, is not divine. Jewish healing formats that allow this affirmation gently to surface help in the task of transcendence, for they remind us that even as we are more than our illnesses, we are also more than our bodies; we "are" also our souls, affirmed by Jewish tradition as eternal.

God As Revealer—Healing of Spirit

When we pray for healing, we pray as well for *refu'at hanefesh*, the healing of the spirit. Some physical afflictions are accompanied by coordinate sickness of the spirit, and some afflictions are of the spirit alone. Sadness, depression, anxiety, and anger are only a few of the maladies that exhaust the soul and diminish its luster. A liberal Jewish theology of healing might rediscover, in the metaphor of God as Revealer, resources that can support and sustain those who seek healing of the spirit.

We know from the biblical accounts of the deliverance from Egypt that among the most difficult challenges, for God as well as for the Israelites, was the eradication of a sense of enslavement. Even after the passage from Egypt, the community seemed unable to imagine itself as anything other than a group of slaves. They remained wedded to the images of oppression and uncertain how to manage the transition to liberation.

The revelation at Sinai intercedes, and from that moment on, potentially at least, the community begins to grasp the possibility of what it might mean to re-image oneself. Put differently, the revelation of God, whatever we might understand that to be, stands as a dividing line between what is and what might be.

A liberal Jewish theology of healing ought to emphasize the dialogic and covenantal dimensions of the revelation at Sinai. For progressive Judaism, what matters is the decisive incursion of God into the life of the community and the covenantal response of that community to their shared experience. Torah emerges out of the call-and-response understanding of revelation affirmed by progressive Judaism.

Revelation As the Possible

Revelation can be an important category for the healing of the spirit. God as revealer can become the spirit/power/dimension of reality on which we depend for the ability to detach from a self-perception as someone who is "sick in spirit," i.e., enslaved by illness. Revelation becomes the incursion into our lives of the divine call to which we respond with "all our heart and all our soul" as we enter into a new relationship that presents the possibilities of the future.

In progressive Judaism, we often reject the traditional metaphor of revelation because we do not expect God to whisper the magic word that will alleviate our illness. But so too must we reject the classical liberal/humanistic view of humans as "godly," which might imply that those who suffer in spirit must somehow "lift themselves."

Revelation-as-relationship is a post-modern insight worth exploring as a means of healing. We need to consider the decisive moment of Sinai as a metaphor for entering into relationship with God, a God who is revealed to us in ongoing dialogue with the soul and spirit. The ancient Israelites had, after all, been freed from the physical constraints of bondage before they reached Sinai; the giving of the Torah is understood by tradition as the beginning of the healing of the spirit of servitude.

The Place of Study

The revelation at Sinai is a revelation of words, which inaugurates a tradition of study as prayer. What a liberal Jewish theology of healing can do to foster *refu'at hanefesh,* healing of spirit, is to create opportunities, primarily of study, in which ancient and modern voices are heard in their response to the reality of God.

In addition to song and meditation, prayer and poetry, our services of healing should thus allow for periods of study, preferably in *chevrutah* (establishing and reinforcing the reality of human contact). We should provide texts that speak of the afflicted soul, and encourage those in need to see these texts as resources in the attempt to establish and maintain a dialogic and covenantal relationship with God.

The Psalms as well as the wisdom literature (particularly Proverbs and Ecclesiastes) contain many examples of insights that help locate us within the larger universe of the Spirit of which we are a part. God as Revealer becomes the partner in the healing of the spirit because, as Revealer, God enters into relationship with the "us" that is more than (but not separate from) body. The literature of the destructions of 586 B.C.E. and 70 C.E., although largely couched in collective terms, also suggests responses which may be beneficial to the individual.

Afflictions of the spirit may not disappear, may not even perhaps diminish (as indeed the imprint of slavery remained on the generation of the Exodus). But in moments of revelation, those who know the suffering of the soul can glimpse a light towards which they may be guided and from which they may draw hope. They can appreciate the illumination that breaks their darkness.

Listening to Voices

Our classical texts and contemporary poetry contain personal testimonials to the ability of the soul and spirit to hear the Voice of God and become transformed in response. And where transformation is not possible, there are also models of transcendence—in the stories of those who were able to see through and past their immediate circumstance to a deeper dimension of life and living. At the risk of minimizing the experience of European Jewry in [the twentieth] century, as well as incorrectly associating illness with genocidal assault, many of the responsa of the Sho'ah (Holocaust) demonstrate a determination to maintain dignity through the affirmation of transcendent value/ritual in situations of extreme distress.

We should not, however, limit ourselves to texts of distress. We need to hear the words of those whose spirits have soared, and whose lives have been whole. Jewish experience, like individual human experience, has witnessed joy as well as sorrow, elevation as well as degradation. We need to remember the blessings of life, and to assert our affirmation for the beauty, love, and creativity that are also part of human existence.

God as Revealer can thus become a source of sustenance to those in need of healing of spirit when we use the myth and metaphor to seek and suggest opportunities for entering into relationship with God.

God As Redeemer—Healing of Wholeness

We end where we begin. We should not forget that the traditional *Mi Sheberakh* for healing begins with the hope of a *refu'ah shelemah*, a healing of wholeness, before it goes on to ask for the healing of body and spirit *(refu'at hanefesh* and *refu'at haguf)*. Ultimately, what we seek in healing is the fusion of body and spirit in the quest for transcendence of circumstance.

Redemption is a problematic metaphor for progressive Judaism. We reject the supernatural narrowness that encapsulates the hope for the future in the personality of an anointed one, a messiah, who will act as God's agent in rectifying the wrongs of life. Yet we need to affirm, as an act of Jewish covenantal faithfulness, the belief in the future that resides within that archaic imagery.

Progressive Jews now understand the problematic assumptions of the once common classical liberal substitute for the Messiah—the "Messianic Era." This imagined time of universal peace and wholeness brought about by corporate human effort was once the glory of a rational faith. [Now], however, faith in universal human goodness seems as irrational as the expected arrival of the Messiah son of David. Neither the Messiah nor the Messianic Era are any longer anticipated with equanimity.

So how then do we bring together the quest for *refu'ah shelemah*, the healing of wholeness, with the affirmation of God as Redeemer? How can a liberal Jewish theology of healing recover meaning from this most difficult of categories?

The Faithful Healer

Reclaiming the attribute of God as Redeemer might become yet another resource in our quest for healing. It is through the act of redemption that God becomes for us the *Rofeh Ne'eman*, the Faithful Healer, for it is through redemption that the inequities and injustices of life and of living are set right. It is through redemption that illness, agony, and yes, even death, are overcome and denied finality. And only with faith in God can we make this final affirmation that becomes the ultimate source of true healing.

What Elisha accomplishes in the mythic story with which this article began is not merely the reanimation of the dead child. Through the symbolic seven-fold sneezing, the primal seven-day act of creation which concludes with God breathing life into Adam, animating and ensouling him at the same moment, is recapitulated. Healing can be, quite literally, giving the gift of life, giving the gift of meaning, giving the gift of reawakening to the blessings that have been bestowed, the reality of which illness and loss cannot revoke.

Redemption becomes the act of experiencing our lives as ultimately being one with the God who is One. It is knowing that the end of living is not the end of life, and believing that beyond illness of body and spirit there is the peace of eternality beneath the wings of the *Shekhinah.* The God who creates the context for living, and who is revealed in the encounter and response of our deepest living, is the God who preserves the holiness of each life that is lived in the world.

Facing Death

Many Jews no longer know that there exists in Jewish liturgy a special *Vidui,* or confessional prayer, to be recited at the end of life. It is an essential tool for the healing of wholeness. This is what a Jew is supposed to say when death approaches: "I acknowledge before You, my God and God of my ancestors, that both my recovery and my death are in Your hand. May it be Your will to send me a complete healing. But if death be Your decree, I will accept it in love from Your hand. . . . Into Your hand I entrust my spirit. . . . *Shema Yisra'el Adonay Eloheynu Adonay Echad;* Listen, People-Of-Which-I-Am-A-Part [and, therefore, I am not alone], *Adonay* Is Our God, *Adonay* Alone."

That trust and love is what we mean when we say "You shall love the Lord your God with all your heart, and with all your soul, and with all your might." A whole heart is one that can still love, despite pain, that can let go without letting go. A healed heart is one which has endured loss—even anticipated and glimpsed its own loss—and can still be filled with meaning. Seeing the boundaries of life, we retain the capacity to transcend them by denying their finality. *Refu'ah shelemah,* healing of wholeness, comes with the understanding that to love God with all of our heart can only mean with everything that is in our lives, the joy and the sadness, the presence and the memory, the health and the sicknesses, the hope and the loss.

The healing of wholeness, as the *Mi Sheberakh* defines it, is the healing of body and the healing of spirit. We should read the prayer thus: *"Refu'ah shelemah*—[this is] *refu'at hanefesh* [together with] *refu'at haguf."* What we pray for, then, is not only the moment of recovery or the lifting of the cloud that rests on our spirit; what we pray for ultimately is to understand our lives within the grand metaphors of creation, revelation, and redemption. What we pray for is incorporation of our individual lives into the eternal life of God, which alone can redeem us.

The Work Ahead

According to the Talmud, "Until the time of Abraham there were no physical signs of aging; until the time of Jacob, no one ever became sick; until Elisha, no one ever became sick and recovered" (B. *Bava Metzia* 87a).

Rabbis—liberal or otherwise—cannot revive the dead, and cannot cure the afflicted. Only God can do the former, and doctors cannot always do the latter. But we can be healers, and we can support healing, because even those who will not recover from a betrayal of the body or spirit by any number of cruel, unjust, and debilitating diseases can be healed.

Liberal Judaism can create a healthy atmosphere for exploring healing from a spiritual perspective. We can provide services, sources, song, and study which support the soul and create community. Rabbis can become spiritual guides, opening up the richness of four millennia of often weary yet triumphant experience with loss and recovery, sickness and health, despair and affirmation.

Not everyone with whom we work is going to "get better." We will experience sadness, loss, impotence, and anger. The ways in which we rabbis respond to our own limitations may be among the most powerful lessons we teach about transcending circumstance and keeping faith. No less than those with whom we work, we require healing in order to remain healers.

And so we pray: "Heal us, *Adonay*, and we shall be healed; save us and we shall be saved, for You are our praise. Grant a healing of wholeness from all our afflictions; for You are a sovereign God and a faithful and compassionate Healer. Praised are You, *Adonay*, who heals the sick among your people Israel, and all the inhabitants of Your world."

A Perspective on Jewish Healing

NAOMI MARK

"How do you do that?" This was the question often posed to me over the last seven years, during which I served as a social worker counseling cancer patients and their families, at Memorial Sloan-Kettering Cancer Center in NYC. Having recently left that job, I now realize that being the non-medical member of an interdisciplinary team of physicians, nurses, and others, did evoke questions for me as well. If healing is not simply physical, then what non-physical (spiritual, emotional, psychological) elements are involved in healing? How can one attempt to assist in the healing of those struggling to cope with catastrophic illness? Given the sometimes insurmountable obstacles facing these patients, what can be done or said that could possibly make things better? What is it that I and other mental health providers, chaplains, and countless others do that qualifies as "Jewish healing"?

Drawing on both therapeutic and Jewish principles, I offer here a conceptual framework and an approach to "healing" for those who are healers and those who are trying to promote healing or offer help to someone who is sick.

"Standing There": The Foundation of Healing

"Don't just stand there—do something!" is the instinctive response one feels upon witnessing others in pain or distress. Within the field of medicine, this motto is the usual practice: order more tests, try different medications, initiate a referral to a related specialist, etc. Often the more dedicated the medical team, the more activity is generated; the intensity and sense of imminent crisis is constant when working with serious illness.

In healing the human spirit, however, "doing something" is often not enough. Dr. David Spiegel, chief of the Department of Psychiatry at Stanford University Hospital and author of many books on his work with cancer patients, therefore, reformulated the maxim, "Don't just do something—stand there!" Being present and "standing there" together with those who are ill is far more difficult than it may initially seem, but it is on this foundation that the healing relationship is forged and it is within this relationship that the healing takes place.

Challenges for Helpers/Caregivers/Healers

1 Identity: "The patient is not the illness"

One of the most difficult aspects of being chronically ill is the way in which others tend to identify the ill person with the illness. We are all familiar with numerous tales of patients who experienced the stripping of their former identifies as they slowly become identified even by those closest to them as the disease which they are fighting to overcome. The illness can often take over the perceptions of hospital staff, families, and tragically, at times that of the ill themselves. Tapping into the many other aspects of personal identity can therefore be restorative. The idea that illness is not to become a total identity, but rather part of a bigger picture, parallels the notion in *halakhah* that the poor are also obligated to give *tzedakah*. They are not to be viewed simply as *poor* people but are entitled to the same privileges and responsibilities of giving as everyone else.

2 Contextualization: Illness as part of the story

When illness is seen in a vacuum, ripped from the context of the entire flow of the ill person's history, it can be more difficult for the ill to cope and to assume control. A sense of shame may develop or increase. Traditional Judaism encourages that the illness be understood as part of the whole picture of one's life, inspiring a change in name, and ultimately a spirit of *teshuvah*.

It can therefore be restorative for the ill to share their stories and to have the illness understood as but one chapter of their life narrative. When provided with a fuller context with which to view the current crisis, the ill person may then be able to integrate this episode into his/her larger sense of self, to let go of the shame/secrecy about the illness and to begin to serve as a model for others on the integration of wellness and sickness in our community.

The feeling of being "broken by the world" is experienced by each of us individually, and depending on our life circumstance, at different thresholds. Yet, as the Kotzker Rebbe taught, there is nothing as whole as a broken heart—demonstrating that the struggle to find healing is more than just an attempt to recapture our former selves, but also a vision of ourselves, even if only for a brief moment, where the broken or fragmented parts have come together to form a new fuller whole.

3 *Existential: "What does this mean? What can I learn?"*

It is my observation that those who are able to find a purpose/meaning/lesson/"benefit" within the illness are better able to cope and to come to terms with the impact of what has happened. This means finding some benefit, some purpose, some transcendence within the experience, a sense of having achieved things out of illness and healing which could otherwise not have been possible. It must be emphasized that the meaning is only to be construed by the ill—and not by the "healer" or anyone else. Interpretations of illness and the responses to suffering are very personal and unique to each circumstance.

This area is particularly delicate as for many, there exists a temptation to be simplistic, to assume an accusatory blaming stance when seeking meaning in illness. As we learned from the tradition's condemnation of Job's comforters (those who said he deserved his suffering as a punishment from God), these formulaic attempts to explain the unexplainable are unacceptable. Illness should never be glibly described as "deserved" or as a tit-for-tat form of punishing. It is difficult to reach for meaning in illness given the many voices today in the political, religious and "new age" worlds, who imply causal relationships between illness and behavior: "I invited it," "It's your fault," etc. These oversimplifications must be rejected. Yet as Victor Frankl suggested, it may be possible to derive personal meaning from suffering and thus transform the pain. For example:

Dr. Mortimer Mark: When my father was diagnosed with a rare, debilitating neurological condition, he (being a physician), at once understood that the prognosis was poor. Though he endured much suffering over the course of the four-year period in which he was sick (describing his situation once as "falling off a mountain in slow motion"), he attempted to use the time, focus, room and intensity provided by the illness to prepare himself for death and (as he believed) for after death and the World-to-Come. He took the chance to re-examine his life, to put his emotional and ethical affairs in order, and to reconcile and heal relationships with family and friends, availing himself of the time given to him for a final crack at recreating and reconstructing himself to be the person he wanted to finally be.

The period during which my father was ill also provided those whom he had loved, helped, cared for over the years with the opportunity to reciprocate that love and to demonstrate their admiration in a way that until the illness was not possible. And the illness made him receptive to it in a way that he would not have been otherwise. This was healing for both.

4 Communal—Reducing Isolation: "I am alone."

The *mi shebeirakh* blessing recited for the sick calls for the person to be healed, along with all fellow Jews who are ill and concludes, "all Jews are connected." The blessing for healing includes others in the community and in the world who are also broken. What is striking about this approach is its negation of the narcissism to which we have become too accustomed, e.g., "My pain is like no other," though the prayer does acknowledge the legitimacy of each person's particular despair. The blessing seeks to provide comfort by letting the sick know that they are still a part of the community, that they are not alone in their pain and confusion. It says that while we live in an unredeemed and broken world, there is comfort in being a part of the collective.

The existential loneliness inherent in the illness process is also reflected in the well-known *gemara* which cites that when one visits the sick, one takes away 1/60 of the illness. Rav Soloveitchik explains that the reduction of each others' loneliness is an ever-present value in Jewish law. In fact, throughout the life cycle, whenever one is expected to feel most alone, the *halakhah* commands that others be present.

Healing, from a Jewish perspective, recognizes the integrity of individual suffering while reminding us that we are part of a collective, with a common thread of existential yearning. And, it is in this attempt to connect to each other and to the "Outstretched Arm," that healing/redemption/transcendence is possible.

Can Prayer Heal?
A View From Tradition

ERICA BROWN

In traditional prayer, three times daily, we supplicate in the plural for "complete healing to all our wounds" to a God who "is a faithful and merciful healer." Yet, this does not stop us from reading between the lines and wondering about the efficacy of such prayer. Is it optimistic but wasted breath? Perhaps in the era when much of our prayer was composed, medical treatment was still in such a primitive state that prayer stood just as much a chance of healing as any other method. But today, in light of medical advances, are we so confident in the power of the word to heal?

There have been medical trials that have attempted to demonstrate that intercessory prayer, even without the patient's knowledge that he or she was the subject, has beneficial effects on medical outcomes.[1] Individual doctors have written persuasively as witnesses of prayer's psychological value and even documented how their own prayers for patients have helped assist in the healing process.[2] But in an age of antibiotics, inoculations and ultrasounds it is hard not to be skeptical. Is prayer supposed to come with any medical guarantees or are its benefits measured differently?

Intercession—Divine or Human?

In the Hebrew Bible, Numbers 12:10–15, we have one of the most beautiful and poignant prayers for recovery. Miriam was stricken with what has been classically called leprosy for slandering her brother Moses. The text reads:

> The cloud had departed from atop the tent and behold! Miriam was afflicted with leprosy like snow. Aaron turned to Miriam and behold! She was afflicted with leprosy. Aaron said to Moses, "I beg you, my lord, do not cast a sin upon us, for we have been foolish and have sinned. Let her not be like a corpse, like one who leaves his mother's womb with half his flesh having been consumed." Moses cried out to God, saying, "Please, God, heal her now." God said to Moses, "Were her father to spit in her face, would she not be humiliated for seven days? Let her be put outside the camp for seven days and then she may be brought in." So Miriam was put outside the camp for seven days and the people did not journey until Miriam was brought in.

This passage is riddled with curiosities. Miriam's challenge to her brother resulted in a heavy punishment, and if biblical punishments are generally commensurate and colored by the crime committed then the reader must struggle with the mystery of Miriam's illness. The repetition of the term "behold" almost forces us to look at Miriam's bodily derangement the way that Aaron himself did. Not all sickness had as crippling an effect on the appearance as did leprosy. Aaron, who participated, even passively, in this crime was left unblemished. As powerful as Moses' prayer was—and it is still evoked every Yom Kippur—God maintained that Miriam had to be punished. The children of Israel waited for Miriam's return and strangely, a narrative which focuses on the intimate details of sibling tension ends with the entire camp involved.

Miriam challenged her brother's authority in the beginning of the chapter. She suggested that she and Aaron were just as capable of communicating with God as Moses was. Yet she did so by unfairly evoking an image of a tarnished husband. Moses desisted from normal domestic relations, according to the midrash (collection of rabbinic interpretations) and several exegetes.[3] His service to God was so demanding that he was freed from the bounds of family life. Miriam was troubled by this and found it indefensible. She and Aaron were also prophets but indulged in their human needs. Did Moses think he was a higher grade prophet than they? But here she questioned not Moses but God's choice of him and the unusual demands God made of him. In addition, she did not focus on the nature of revelation but on Moses's intimate personal life, one that she had no right to question.

Slander by its nature is a public activity, even if that public is limited to one. By slandering her brother, she tried to promote some defect in his character to someone else. In turn, the commensurate punishment would be to experience some form of public deformity. Leprosy is described in detail in Leviticus. It was an illness with very visible signs. The passage itself is very visual and the repetition of the term "behold" in verse ten alerts us to the shock of looking at the leper. The slow movement of Aaron turning and witnessing his sister in this state is recorded twice. The text narrates it and then the reader experiences it with Aaron as he sees his beloved sister in physical anguish. Based on this visceral reaction, Aaron pleads with Moses not to let this dignified leader look like a stillborn child in front of the entire encampment.

Moses Feinstein, a leading Orthodox rabbi, was asked if one could fulfill the commandment to visit the sick with a phone call.[4] He demurred to the convenience of the telephone and admitted that it may provide some comfort. However, he advised that not only is there more commiseration with a visit but that unless an individual actually sees his friend in pain, he will not adequately pray for him. The visual enhancement of seeing a sick person will inspire more powerful prayer. This is clearly demonstrated in our narrative.

Did Aaron also suffer this affliction? The Talmud is, as expected, divided on the matter.[5] One camp claims that the text does not confess Aaron's punishment so it must have been withheld or undeserved. It is Miriam in the text who speaks. The other camp claims that for his participation in the discussion, even as passive listener, he received the same punishment. Why not mention it? Aaron could very well have had leprosy but that is not what the text wants to emphasize. It is his shock and mercy that are paramount here. If Aaron were ill that would only highlight the beauty of his concern: despite his own illness, he beseeched Moses to cure his sister.

Why did Aaron not turn to God himself? Here, it is important to see the text as a composite and not in a line-by-line reading. God had just stridently informed Aaron and Miriam that Moses' prophecy was superior to theirs. Thus, when it came to communicating with God, Aaron humbled himself before his younger brother. Notice the appellation Aaron attached to his speech, "I beg you, my lord . . ." instead of "I beg you, my brother." Aaron had learned his lesson.

But Miriam evidently had not. One medieval commentator remarked that the whiteness brought on by the illness was the price she paid for accusing Moses of taking a dark-skinned woman as wife. Her whiteness now was not something to be proud of but the extreme coloring or absence of color that was a badge of shame. It was as branding as any mark Hawthorne could assign. Had she insulted her father she would have been publicly humiliated, all the more so, when she called into question the divine mechanics of the universe. God chose Moses; who was she to question? She tried to slander her brother, to put him metaphorically outside the camp, so she had to be put outside the camp herself.

Sickness as Isolation

Being put outside the camp was essentially a heightened form of the illness itself. Sickness is isolating. Being exiled is merely an exacerbated form of the same anguish—isolation. Pain isolates because it makes you acutely aware of yourself, often blinded to the pain of others because of the intensity of personal anguish. This self-focus is itself a punishment. Wittgenstein, the famous 20th century philosopher, wrote convincingly about the deficiency of language to convey pain because even when we confess similar illness to a friend, relative or colleague, we know that the way we experience toothaches, sprains, and splinters is unique to ourselves. Pain is very individualized. "Both of us cry, contort our faces, give the same description of the pain, etc. Now are we to say we have the same pain or different ones?"[6]

When we gossip, we are not thinking about ourselves. We focus on the blemishes of others. When we are sick, especially with an illness which has physically unpleasant manifestations, we think only about ourselves.

Miriam was alienated by a very public sickness. What cured her? It was not the prayer of her brother. God refused his request. It was knowing that her brothers prayed for her. But it was more. The narrative ends with the resumption of Israel's sojourns in the wilderness. The camp waits for her. The same camp from which she has been excluded inconveniences itself for an entire week to wait for her healing. The very brother she insulted petitioned God for her recovery. What cured her was not prayer, since God told Moses that she must not be spared punishment, but the almost unconditional love that inspired prayer. If sickness is isolating on one level it is also embracing on another. We stop thinking about ourselves when others think about us.

A Response to Others

We do not get better because we have responsibilities to others that only we can fulfill but because we want to better enjoy the love that others have displayed while we were ill. In a room filled with flowers and cards, when several people a day visit and ask for our Hebrew names so that they may gently suggest divine assistance, we heal through love. Moses taught his sister that although she may not have been thinking kindly of him, he still prayed for her. Aaron healed his sister by expressing such personal anguish at her suffering. The children of Israel healed Miriam because they waited for her.

We do not know what the answers to our prayers are. Maybe they will be no. We cannot pray audaciously expecting a change in divine will. It is the prayer itself which must ultimately concern us, the way it molds our character, the way it forms our concern for others, the way we demonstrate to the sick that our love may help carry them to good health. In that capacity it is healing. In a touching personal essay on being the recipient of such prayer, a woman struggling with cancer wrote of hearing that someone prayed on her behalf, ". . . I was overwhelmed. This woman whom I barely knew, had said my name and prayed for me every day for months. It was a great gift. . . . And it is good for the person who is ill to know that we are praying on their behalf, so that through the act of praying, they will feel the love of the community embracing them in their hour of need. And in the process, please God, it helps all of us feel God's care more deeply as well."[7]

We should not be seduced by medical statistics on prayer's efficacy. Prayer is not medicine, nor is it meant to be. Unlike medicine, it cannot be taken; it can only be given. It cannot be mechanical; it must be personal. Prayer is not a prevention for pain nor its cure; it is a response to pain. It is the emotional, intimate recordings and reflections of Miriam outside the camp, the vociferous pleadings of her brothers inside the camp, and the patient wait of the entire camp that inspired prayer and ultimately began the healing process. Love that inspires prayer inspires healing.

Notes

1. See, for example, the 1988 study done by Dr. Randolph C. Byrd entitled, "Positive Therapeutic Effects of Intercessory Prayer in a Coronary Care Unit Population" (*Southern Medical Journal:* July, 1988, vol. 8, no. 7). He concludes there that the "data suggest that intercessory prayer to the Judeo-Christian G-d has a beneficial therapeutic effect in patients admitted to a CCU." Other interesting studies include "The Efficacy of Prayer: A Double Blind Clinical Trial" in the *Journal of Chronic Disease* 18:367–377, 1965 and P.J. Collipp, "The Efficacy of Prayer: A Triple Blind Study" in *Medical Times* 97:201–204, 1969. These studies have aroused some controversy as to the clinical methods used to derive the positive conclusions.

2. In one such publication, *Healing Words* by Dr. Larry Dossey, the writer describes the difficulty in praying for the outcome of his patient given that a simple prayer for recovery did not necessarily match the complexity of the diagnosis or the needs of the patient or his or her family. His prayer was reduced to a simple formula "May the best possible outcome prevail" in the hope that this would make him more attuned to the patient's individual needs.

3. *Midrash Tanhuma* 96:13 as cited by Rashi, *Sifrei Ba'alotekha* 99. See also BT Bava Batra 109b. These midrashim are not an indictment of Moshe as much as they demonstrate sympathy with Zipporah's difficult position.

4. R. Moshe Feinstein, *Iggerot Moshe*, Y.D. I, #223.

5. Babylonian Talmud, Shabbat 97a.

6. Ludwig Wittgenstein, *The Blue and Brown Books: Preliminary Studies for the "Philosophical Investigations"* (New York: 1958), p. 54.

7. Elana Kanter, *The Healing Power of Prayer*, p. 28:554, 1998.

Overcoming Our Pain
The Life Lessons of Dr. Bernie S. Siegel

ARON HIRT-MANHEIMER

*D*r. *Bernie S. Siegel, a surgeon and author of the best-seller* Love, Medicine, & Miracles, *as well as* Peace, Love, and Healing *and* How to Live Between Office Visits, *found peace and love in his own life after a transformative experience that helped him become a healer par excellence. He spoke with* [Reform Judaism *magazine*] *editor Aron Hirt-Manheimer about his personal awakening and how all of us can prevail over disease.*

What induced you to make the transition from conventional surgeon to healer?

What changed me was my feelings of pain and unhappiness, and my awareness of the inadequacies of our medical profession, which is focused on disease, not on the people you're taking care of and not on the person who's giving the care.

Many doctors are suffering from post-traumatic stress disorder. They have no way to deal with feelings. If I amputated a patient's wrong leg and wanted to talk about how I felt at a complications conference, my colleagues would respond: Don't tell us how you feel; tell us what you think we can do to avoid this happening again.

I went into medicine for healthy reasons. I like people and wanted to help them. But at the same time I felt intense unhappiness and pain because you can't cure everybody and because the medical establishment wasn't teaching me how to deal with my feelings.

Out of that pain I made the effort to seek help. I went to a few doctor/patient workshops to teach me how to handle my feelings and those of my patients, and to gain some new tools to enable myself and them to heal. At one of the workshops a patient said to me, "You're a nice guy and I feel better when I'm in your office, but I can't take you home with me. So how do I live between office visits?" Her statement hit me like a bolt of lightning. I thought, wait a minute, I need to know how to live, too.

Ironically, when I first started attending these workshops in 1977, I was skeptical of the presenters and their techniques. But then I had these incredible experiences. In my first encounter with Carl Simonton, a pioneer in guided imagery, he said to our group, close your eyes. Well, I wasn't going to do it. The doctor in me said, this is nuts. But I was sitting in the front row and he was looking straight at me. I didn't have the courage to stare back at him. So I shut my eyes, thinking he won't know I'm faking it. But I'm so visual that as soon as he started talking about an inner guide, I started seeing one.

Tell us what you saw.

Being a doctor with an ego, I expected my imaginary inner guide to be Abraham, Moses, or someone of equal importance. Well, coming down the path was this guy in his 30s, wearing sandals, a beard, and a hat that looked like a pillbox or a fez. He said, I'm George.

After that, George would speak to me about things both simple and sublime. One day he said, "You're a doctor, look at your clothes. You need a new wardrobe." I started laughing because he was right. His comments would come whether I wanted to hear them or not. I didn't create the conversation; George was just there, talking to me, and he's been with me ever since. Later, I found an old photograph of my father's bearded grandfather. And what was he wearing on his head? The same hat that George wears, which I discovered was an old style of yarmulke.

So George is your inner voice.

Yes. And the voice is available to all of us, if we learn how to listen to it. It doesn't have to be quiet outside—you can hear God in New York City too, but one must take the time to listen to the voice.

What did the voice teach you about yourself as a doctor?

It helped me to become myself. I dreamt one night that a young man (whom I knew was me) walked up to me, took me in his arms, and said thank you for letting us out. I knew what he was saying was thanks for taking the lid off and letting us out of unconsciousness, thanks for paying attention to your dreams and what's inside of you. Most of all, the voice helped me release what had been stored up in me, that stuff which becomes an illness itself if it's not released. After that experience, I was ready for anything. If my family, a patient, or a nurse was critical of me, I said, tell me why. If I needed to improve what kind of a father, husband, or doctor I was, I said, tell me how.

By liberating yourself, were you able to then change your relationship with your patients? Because you could see their pain, could you better help them help themselves?

I became a person. Before that, I had been Dr. Siegel, but I didn't know who I was. When I became Bernie, a human being who acknowledged my own troubles and feelings, and realized they were the same experiences a lot of others were having, I was able to help people as a fellow human being rather than as the authority figure. I listened to people because I didn't have answers. They got better because I let them empty themselves out.

So you became a combination of therapist, spiritual guide, and doctor. You began to practice "clergery," as your wife put it.

I'd say a storyteller too, because I learned the power of images and hypnotherapy from the writings of Carl Jung, Milton Erickson, and Joseph Campbell, among others. Information alone doesn't help people. People know what's good for them and don't do it. What you have to do is inspire them. When they become inspired, then they're open to revelation, to pursuing the meaning of life. One piece of information that often changes people is learning that they are going to be dead in twelve months. After the revelation comes the transformation.

According to your books, spiritual people have a higher recovery rate. Why?

The long-term survivors, those who beat the odds, all have certain traits in common. They have the ability to show anger. They don't accept a diagnosis that declares they will be dead in two months. They get mad and start fighting. They refuse to see themselves as victims. They buy books, go to workshops, change themselves. They also call on God. True peace of mind comes when you have a divine source to help, support, and accompany you, to get you through difficulties and to show you the strength you really have. A relationship with God can help you overcome things that defeat other people.

Does prayer help?

Personally, I don't ask God to take away illness or pain. I say, show me the way, the strength, guide me. Take the lid off so I know what inner resources I have. During prayer you are willing to look into the darkness, to go into the deeper level inside yourself, and to learn things that can help you get through whatever is happening.

So you help people find doorways into their inner selves.

Yes. But most people turn down my invitation to join our groups. I think they are afraid of revealing their emotions. Only a minority of people are willing to let out their feelings in order to fight a disease. My wife, Bobbie, calls them "exceptional" patients. Everyone is capable of being exceptional, but only a few are willing to take that step.

You've said, "fatalism can be fatal." How important is hope?

If you take hope away, people die. It's physiological. Despair affects the immune system by changing the chemical environment in the body. If you're anticipating death, you're suppressing your immune system; conversely, if you anticipate survival, you're enhancing your ability to fight disease and your lines of defense are love, joy, and laughter.

People call this type of healing miraculous. Is it really?

Whenever people experience a miracle and I ask them how they managed it, invariably they give me a list of what they did. The peo-

ple who have had a miraculous healing will tell you it wasn't an accident. It may be a miracle, but they participated in it.

Do you find that doctors by and large have been open to your ideas?
They used to say, "it's not scientific" or "you're creating guilt."
Now they are not arguing with me because a lot of research has con-
firmed what I discovered intuitively.

*We've talked about medicine and miracles. The other word in the
title of your first book is "love." Why is love so important in
healing?*
Love is the most potent stimulant of the human immune system.
Joy and laughter are great, but the most powerful physiological state
is the loving state. Psychiatrist Paul Menninger says that love helps
two people: the person you're extending it to and the person giving it.
And it has an effect on everyone around you. We're all changed by
love.

*You've observed that, for many patients, belief in a loving, caring
God is an important element in recovery. What kind of messages can
we receive from God?*
The first is "Don't feel personally, irrevocably, eternally responsible
for everything. That's God's job." The second is "Everything you
remember God forgets, everything you forget God remembers." The
third is "If you go around saying, 'I've got a miserable life,' God says,
'You think that's miserable, let me show you what miserable is.' If you
go around saying, 'I've got a wonderful life,' God says, 'I'll show you
what a wonderful life really is.'" And the fourth is "I love you, just the
way you are."

Healing of Body; Healing of Spirit

RABBI NANCY FLAM

Serious illness affronts the whole person: body, mind and spirit. Early on, Jewish liturgy acknowledged that the ill person seeks healing on different levels. In our central prayer for healing, the *mi shebeirakh,* we pray for a complete healing: *refuah shleima.* The prayer then specifies what is meant by a complete healing: *refuat haguf,* the healing of the body, or what we sometimes refer to as "cure," and *refuat hanefesh,* the healing of the spirit, the soul, the self. Modern western medicine mainly addresses our need for physical healing. However, at the same time as we seek physical health, we also seek spiritual healing in response to the assaults not to our body, but to our person: emotional upheaval, social dislocation, and spiritual discomfort.

I am a rabbi, not a physician. When I talk about "Jewish healing," I refer to the spiritual, not physical dimension of healing. I speak of how the Jewish tradition and community achieves (or helps another person achieve) a sense of spiritual well-being, wholeness, perspective, fulfillment or comfort, especially around issues of illness, suffering and loss.

The key traditional Jewish resources for spiritual healing are the three pillars of Judaism itself: *Torah* (the study of Jewish texts), *avodah* (prayer) and *gemilut hassadim* (acts of loving kindness). As Jews, these practices are always at the core of our spiritual life. However, when we are confronted with serious illness, we refract these practices through a particular lens, and in so doing discover the Jewish genius of *refuat hanefesh.* In reverse order, I explore these resources below.

Gemilut Hassadim

Perhaps the central healing practice which the tradition teaches is the *mitzvah* of *bikkur holim,* visiting those who are ill. There is a natural tendency toward isolation at times of illness. Not only are we often physically displaced from our usual roles as workers, parents and community members, but we often experience psychological isolation as well. The *mitzvah* of *bikkur holim* mitigates the existential aloneness and abandonment that illness often brings.

The core of the *mitzvah* is to be with someone and to be present, to provide company and to share some of the burden by empathically carrying it just a bit. In the world of pastoral care, this actually has a name. It is called "the ministry of presence." We offer our full attention and our full love to the one we are visiting without our own agenda interfering, without expectation. We are just together in the moment. Our hope is that our loving presence will convey a sense of God's own loving presence.

Avodah

The second main Jewish resource for one who is ill is *avodah:* prayer or worship in its broadest context. By *avodah,* I mean to suggest such activities as individual and communal prayer, meditation, and the spiritual practice of offering *berakhot* (blessings).

Prayer is an essential spiritual tool to use at a time of illness. It is a natural tool. During a hard time, we need to engage our capacity to hope. Prayer allows us an opportunity to articulate our hopes for healing, for cessation from suffering, for blessing to break through in the midst of pain.

Prayer is also what we do when we do not know what to do, when we are aware that our well-being is not entirely in our control. In this sense, prayer can help us acknowledge that our lives are indeed *b'yado,* in God's hands.

Prayer can be a refuge, an inner sanctuary where we find retreat from procedures, treatments and all of the outer world with its many demands. We may find a sense of calm through prayer, a kind of "time out" for reflection.

In addition, when we pray in community and use traditional Jewish liturgy, we not only benefit from the company of others, but we find comfort in knowing that the words we speak have been spoken by millions of others who, like us, yearn for healing.

Meditation is a wonderful resource, as well. Chanting a *niggun* (wordless tune) over and over again can help calm us and connect us to the Source of peace and comfort. Meditating on a particular verse from the Bible or from the *siddur* can help us embody its meaning in a full way.

Saying blessings can help us lift and savor what is beautiful in the moment. We have blessings for pleasures of taste, sight and smell; blessings of gratitude for being in the presence of someone wise, or someone disfigured. In the latter case, we thank God for creating many kinds of human beings. We have a whole list of blessings for getting up in the morning, so that our waking routine does not begin with a slam of the alarm clock, but rather with words of gratitude for simple miracles, such as opening our eyes, stretching, standing up.

It is also possible to use old blessings in new contexts, to sanctify the experience of receiving chemotherapy, of meeting with one's doctor, of doing artificial insemination. The spiritual genius about blessings is that they help us reframe our experience in the context of divine reality.

Torah

Finally, *Torah* study, in its broadest sense, is an excellent spiritual resource for those who are ill. Study of traditional Jewish texts and commentary is, of course, a fundamental pillar of Jewish religious life. Through Torah study we attempt to understand God's will for us. Through study we can connect with God.

Thinking about what God has to do with illness, suffering and healing is an essential cognitive resource. Cognitive resources are just as important as non-cognitive resources (such as prayer, or having another person to be present to us). The reason for this importance is perhaps best explained by analogy. It is well-known that experiencing physical pain without knowing the cause often magnifies the experience of the pain itself. Once we get a diagnosis, particularly if the diagnosis is not life-threatening, it often happens that the physical sensations of pain are more bearable.

It is similar with emotional and spiritual suffering. If we can find or develop a framework with which to understand our suffering, then sometimes the suffering itself becomes more bearable.

Therefore, one may search the tradition and find comfort from any of a number of perspectives: the perspective of Torah that states that good is requited with good, and bad with bad; the perspective of the Wisdom literature which underscores the grand mystery underlying creation; early rabbinic suggestions that justice is meted out in the world to come or that suffering may come to offer us an opportunity to do *teshuvah;* contemporary rabbinic theologies which do not hold God responsible for suffering but rather see God's role as the source of hope, etc. At any one time, we may resonate with one or another perspective. Studying the tradition equips us with knowledge that can help us think about our suffering and search for healing.

Conclusion

Torah, avodah, and *gemilut hassadim,* the central pillars of Jewish practice, are indeed the central resources a Jew uses toward spiritual healing at a time of illness. These practices, which at all times form the basis of a Jew's spiritual life lived deeply, can be refracted through the lens of someone living with serious illness to yield great treasures.

Babylonian Talmud,[*]
Berakhot 5b

"A drug may be beneficial for one person and not for another, but the Torah is a life-giving medicine for all Israel." (R. Judah ben Hiyya, Talmud Eruvin 54a)

[*As a community, we join to support one another in times of illness and loss. Here are several contemporary comments about a piece of classical "healing" text from the Talmud (Tractate* Berakhot *or "Blessings," 5b) that we can use to study together.*]

Rabbi Hiyya bar Abba fell ill and Rabbi Johanan went in to visit him. He [R. Johanan] said to him: "Are your sufferings welcome to you?" He replied: "Neither they nor their reward." He [R. Johanan] said to him: "Give me your hand." He gave him his hand and he [R. Johanan] raised [healed] him.

Rabbi Johanan once fell ill and Rabbi Hanina went in to visit him. He [R. Hanina] said to him: "Are your sufferings welcome to you?" He replied: "Neither they nor their reward." He said to him: "Give me your hand." He [R. Hanina] gave him his hand and he raised him. Why could not R. Johanan raise himself? They replied: "The prisoner cannot free himself from jail."

Rabbi Eleazar fell ill and Rabbi Johanan went in to visit him. He [R. Johanan] noticed that he [R. Eleazar] was lying in a dark room, and he [R. Johanan] bared his arm and light radiated from it. Thereupon he noticed that R. Eleazar was weeping, and he said to him: "Why do you weep? Is it because you did not study enough Torah? Surely we learnt: The one who sacrifices much and the one who sacrifices little have the same merit, provided that the heart is directed to heaven. Is it perhaps lack of sustenance? Not everybody

[*]The Talmud (literally study) is a vast organic compendium of opinions and teachings of ancient Jewish scholars over a period of some eight centuries (from 300 B.C.E. to 500 C.E.). It consists of two parts, the text *(Mishnah)* and related discussion *(Gemara)*, and includes both legal *(Halakhah)* and narrative *(Aggadah)* elements. The Talmud is subdivided into sections known as "tractates." Tractate *Berakhot* ("Blessings") is the first of these and deals generally with the laws regarding prayers and blessings. But by page 5, the rabbis are heavily engaged in a searching discussion concerning the meaning and purpose of suffering. These stories reflect a part of that discussion.

has the privilege to enjoy two tables. Is it perhaps because of the [lack of] children? This is the bone of my tenth son!"—He [R. Eleazar] replied to him: "I am weeping on account of this beauty that is going to rot in the earth." He said to him: "On that account you surely have a reason to weep." And they both wept. In the meanwhile he [R. Johanan] said to him: "Are your sufferings welcome to you?"—He replied: "Neither they nor their reward." He said to him: "Give me your hand." And he gave him his hand and he raised him . . . .

CAROL P. HAUSMAN, PH.D.

What does the question "Are your sufferings beloved or meaningful to you?" mean?

This question means something like "Have you reached the spiritual and psychological point of acceptance, growth, and the ability to be more mindful of your blessings?"

In a spiritual support group for people living with illness, an elderly woman who had a marked, painful limp announced one day that she had decided to love her shortened leg. She began rubbing cream on it every night and speaking tenderly to it. Were her sufferings welcome to her?

Were she then to grow in some important way—become empathic to other disabled people, involved in *tzedekah,* or filled with more lovingkindness—would that mean that her sufferings were welcome to her? Were she even to realize how much she has for which to thank God despite her bad luck, and keep her blessings in mind more of the time, would she welcome her sufferings?

Since the answer in our text is, "neither they nor their reward," the sufferer is offered the healing power of community, *bikkur holim,* study and empathy to help him reach that point of transformation.

DINAH JACOBS

What do you hear in the reply "neither they nor their reward"?

This reply, "Neither the sufferings nor their rewards are welcome to me," emanates from the shattered physical level we are stuck at when we are ill—broken—distant from G-d. We understandably cry about our pain and physical mortality. We are locked within our own jail.

Yet within this shattering, we can be reached by another's out-stretched arm and healing touch, and be lifted and healed. We may not be cured in the physical sense, but in reconnecting to the Source of All Life, we can heal emotionally and spiritually. We move from fragmentation to unity, to *shalom*. *Bikkur Holim*, reaching out to someone within his or her illness, is truly participating in *tikkun olam*, partnering with God to repair the world.

RABBI DR. MEIR SENDOR

In the third story, how do you interpret the nature of the light which radiates from R. Johanan's bared arm?

Sometimes a glowing arm is just a glowing arm. The phenomenon of a perceived luminosity of the human body, or even of other living beings, is well attested in biblical and talmudic sources, and throughout later medieval and modern Jewish mystical traditions. Moshe's face shone in a manner visible to all after his sojourn on Mount Sinai. In the Talmud tractates *Horiot* 12a and *Keritot* 5b–6a there is reference to a technique for perceiving one's own aura in a darkened room. In Lurianic *Kabbalah* and later in the Hasidic tradition, aura gazing was a central diagnostic technique used as an aid in physical and spiritual healing.

When R. Johanan went to visit R. Eleazar, depressed on his sickbed in a dark house, he exposed his glowing arm. An aura can be seen under any lighting conditions, but it is especially striking in the dark, as the *Gemara Horlot* suggests. In showing R. Eleazar how to see the glowing of his arm, R. Johanan helps R. Eleazar make a perception and attitude shift, essential as a first step in healing, helping rouse R. Eleazar out of his depression. This new mode of perception assists his attunement to R. Johanan's own healthy energy field, preparing R. Eleazar to receive the therapeutic hand of R. Johanan directly, and rise up from his bed, whole and healed. . . .

RABBI JOSEPH OZAROWSKI

In the third story, what is the nature of the questions asked by R. Johanan?

In this story, the text reveals two therapeutic approaches. First, we see that the word "notice" (in Aramaic, *haza* and *hazaiah*) is used twice. This demonstrates R. Johanan's awareness of R. Eleazar's condition. He notes the darkened conditions of the room, and he bares his arm to light it up (subject for another *drasha!*). Then he notices R. Eleazar weeping ("seeing sounds" is not unheard of: see Exodus 10:15, where after the Sinaitic revelation, the people "saw the voices").

Secondly, R. Johanan uses questions to zero in on R. Eleazar's suffering, and uses techniques of empathy to connect with and comfort him. He probes three areas:

1. Are intellectual/religious issues bothering you? With regard to learning, the Torah itself values quality over quantity. R. Johanan uses the term *shaninu* . . . meaning "surely <u>we</u> learnt together," attempting to form an empathic and sensitive connection with his colleague, R. Eleazar.
2. Are there livelihood issues? Well, not everyone (including R. Johanan himself) gets rich (the analogy of the two tables).
3. As far as suffering goes, having buried ten children, R. Johanan can truly empathize with R. Eleazar. He, too, has known suffering and loss.

DEBORAH BUCKLEY

What do we learn from the differences between the second story and the first story?

I am fascinated in both stories with what seems to be a formula for Jewish healing:

The question, are sufferings welcome?
The answer, neither they nor reward.
The beckoning, give me your hand.
The giving of the hand and subsequent raising up.

To me, the answer conveys a sense of surrender, a lack of investment in the illness, a place of equanimity that is a requirement for healing. Many times, I cannot surrender when ill, but rather find myself in spiritual and emotional turmoil. The presence of a friend helps lift me out of the depths of pain and suffering to give me new perspective and help carry me to the other side of the dark place, to attain healing.

DR. ALAN B. ASTROW, M.D.

What does the statement "a prisoner can't free himself from jail" mean?

This story calls to mind the experience of the late Dr. Franz Ingelfinger, former editor of the *New England Journal of Medicine.* Ingelfinger was one of the world's leading authorities on diseases of the stomach and esophagus and then tragically and ironically, developed a cancer at the point where the stomach and esophagus connect.

As Ingelfinger recounted, "I can hardly imagine a more informed patient. . . . At that point I received from physician friends throughout the country a barrage of well-intentioned but contradictory advice. As a result, not only I, but my wife, my son, and daughter-in-law (both doctors) became increasingly confused and emotionally distraught. Finally, when the pangs of indecision had become nearly intolerable, one wise physician friend said, 'What you need is a doctor.'. . . When that excellent advice was followed, my family and I sensed immediate and immense relief. The incapacity of enervating worry was dispelled and I could return to my usual anxieties, such as deciding on the fate of manuscripts or giving lectures like this one."

Ingelfinger's experience, though separated from R. Johanan's by almost two millennia, is nevertheless strikingly similar and suggests a quality to illness that transcends time and space. Ingelfinger was one of the great physicians of his era just as R. Johanan was one of the great healers of his, yet each became not only physically but also spiritually incapacitated by disease. Both stories remind us that the sick often feel trapped and isolated by illness and that healing begins with an acknowledgment of our common human frailty. For both the doctor and the rabbi, liberation and reconnection required the warmth of human concern.

Our bodies, source of our individuality and our proud ability when healthy, are painful reminders when we fall ill of how much we need each other. The role of the healer, then, is not just to dispense accurate information, but to serve as the community's agent of reconnection, providing a stable, caring and trustworthy presence when life threatens to spin out of control.

FRANCES BRANDT

In the first story we see a simple model of a successful visit. What went right?

Illness and suffering are lonely experiences, isolating the patient even from those nearby.

By extending one's hand to the stricken person we build a bridge which helps to establish contact and provides a way for the ill person to find their way back to the surrounding world.

This facilitates healing of the spirit and allows the body to heal, also.

RABBI NANCY FLAM

In the third story, R. Johanan poses three questions to R. Eleazar. What did R. Eleazar's answer to these questions accomplish?

R. Eleazar's answer initiated the pivotal moment at which healing could begin. As a person doing the mitzvah of *bikkur holim* knows, creating a relationship of empathic connection is central to healing. However, in this case, the visitor (R. Johanan) was unsuccessful in creating an empathic connection to the person he was visiting (R. Eleazar). Rather than <u>listening</u> for the truth of R. Eleazar's suffering, R. Johanan voiced his own conjectures, thereby frustrating the possibility of creating the groundwork for such a healing relationship. R. Eleazar's reply, surely sharpened by his state of illness, reflects that he was deeply aware of both the exquisite beauty of creation (symbolized by R. Johanan) and the truth that all such beauty passes away. At the moment that R. Eleazar voiced his thoughts, he was able to create the empathic connection that R. Johanan had been unable to foster. Hearing his friend's words, R. Johanan knew not only that R. Eleazar was crying in awareness of life's finitude, but also that R. Johanan himself was part of the miracle of creation that would one day pass away. "Visitor" and "visitee" are always <u>both</u> human, mortal, and vulnerable. R. Eleazar was able to create a relationship of <u>mutual</u> empathy, the partners linked by their mutual awareness of their own mortality. Only then could a truly healing relationship begin.

RABBI SIMKHA Y. WEINTRAUB

In the first story, what do we learn from the interaction between R. Hiyya and R. Johanan?

R. Johanan offered R. Hiyya the crucial opportunity to express something—anything—about how he was doing with, and what meaning he was making of, his suffering. Then, he didn't challenge R. Hiyya's forthright and honest response, which certainly contrasted markedly with some of the pious notions about suffering that were being articulated in the *yeshiva* academy in those days (such as the idea that sufferings were God's "chastisements of love"). Finally, R. Johanan gave R. Hiyya the opportunity to hold hands, to reach back to the one reaching out, if he was so inclined, joining him in simple "post-verbal" human presence, physically re-forging a link with the community of the "temporarily well" while maintaining a position of autonomy, efficacy, and choice for the one who is suffering.

JANICE S. ROUS

Each story ends by the person who is ill being "raised" or "healed" by touch. How do you understand this part of the story?

As a body worker, I am struck by the fact that the person who is ill responds each time by giving the healer his hand. By this act he signifies that he is willing to be healed, which in my experience is crucial to the healing process. Through touch, the person who is ill and the healer enter into a dynamic partnership. The work of the healer is not to take on the pain of the other, but to offer an experience of reconnection, thereby "raising" the person who is ill to a different level of understanding.

II

PERSONAL
STORIES
OF HEALING

Illness Is My Teacher

RABBI NANCY WECHSLER-AZEN

Eight years ago, when I was 26, I was hit by a cab as I crossed a Manhattan street. The left side of my skull was crushed, my face disfigured. I lost vision in my left eye and my sense of smell.

I do not know if what happened to me was providential. I do know that the event changed my life by deepening my compassion for those who hurt. It also strengthened my connection to God through prayer. No, I did not want the pain, the shame, the disfigurement, the emotional and physical scars; but because it happened, I possess the lessons. In the struggle for spiritual awareness, I have become conscious of the many forms in which God communicates with me.

In the intensive care unit of Bellevue Hospital I felt at peace, protected. I never felt punished or out of control. I knew even then that the accident would be a profound teacher. God was telling me that it was time to stop, time to rest, time to be healed, time to receive love from good people, time to become aware. I was given a gift: learning the lessons of life by coming close to death, staying alive in order to share my love and my Torah.

I am integrating the experience of the accident and 15 reconstructive surgeries that ensued into my psyche in such a way that "the car accident" has become part of me just as other experiences are a part of me. This is who I am. Period.

The accident deprived me of the pretty mask I had previously presented to the world. Through the changed appearance, I had to confront what was "really" real; in the process of examining who I was, a new mask took form.

I hate having my picture taken. I am still self-conscious about the outer mask. Yet, the person I am today is in many ways happier than the person who wore my earlier face. Since there is no way out of this duality, I have accepted that there is only a way in.

How did I find the strength to heal during the first months of trauma and years of reconstruction? The keys, I believe, were an iron will and a strong focus. I wanted more than anything else to attend rabbinical school at HUC-JIR, just having transferred from the cantorial program. I was determined to keep my body and my mind fit and healthy. And so I picked myself up after each surgery, took painkillers when needed, put on a bright scarf, and told myself, "do it." Due to fatigue, my ability to concentrate often flagged and I suffered from depression, but my determination was without limit.

Pity brings me down. After the accident I received a letter from a rabbi of my childhood. "Dearest Nancy," he wrote, "I wish that I could sit beside you and hold your hand in the hospital. I would cry with you and share your pain." I did not appreciate his sentiments. Pain is a very private experience. I felt he was responding to a physical mask and not my spirit. I did not want that kind of attention. I wanted upbeat scarves around my head, which was frequently shorn, and colorful cards to decorate the walls of my hospital room. I wanted to watercolor, to listen to healing tapes.

I found great solace in prayer. I prayed with my Muslim and Baptist nurses. I practiced visualization with a friend. On a surgery day I wore a little note taped to my gown saying: "Good morning. God bless all of us during this surgery." And I drew a picture of a mug filled with steaming coffee.

I approached each operation with confidence, though realizing my vulnerability. I received immeasurable support from family, friends, and my doctors. In many ways, these experiences were joyful.

"Coming out" to the congregation about my car accident has brought me healing. I speak about the myth of imperfection, walking forward step by step, lifting blessings from challenges, and the journey from shame to acceptance. My openness and projection of love for those in pain has made it possible for members to approach me. I am a safe haven.

I view May 1, 1985 as my rebirth day, as my personal Purim. On the first day of May, I was taken to the depth and given a new life script. Each time I visit Manhattan, I pay homage—a wink, a quiet smile—offer a prayer of thanksgiving, and stand in awe at that sacred corner, my rebirthplace.

HIRSHEL JAFFE

In 1978 I ran the New York City marathon wearing a t-shirt that identified me as "The Running Rabbi." As we crossed the Verrazano
Narrows Bridge into Brooklyn, chasidim were staring at me and saying in Yiddish, "That's a rabbi?" When I got over the 59th Street
Bridge my wife Judy, daughters Rachel and Nina, and friends Rabbi
Jim and Marsha Rudin cheered me on. I made the V-sign for victory.
I felt indestructible. Little did I realize that in just four years they
would be cheering me on in a different kind of marathon—a race for
my life.

By the Spring of 1982 I began to question my diminishing stamina
during runs. Was I getting old? A few weeks later I couldn't even walk
a quarter of a block. In early June I went to the hospital for tests.

My hemotologist gave me the grim news: "Rabbi Jaffe, we are vir-
tually certain that you have a rare form of leukemia." Summoning my
fighting spirit, my running spirit, I inquired. "How long do people live
with this disease?" He replied, "Six months, a year, five years." I said,
"I'll take the upper limit, doctor."

My treatment began with a spleenectomy. The operation did not go
as well as we had hoped. My blood counts bounced back a little, but
I suffered from a blockage in my intestines. They had to resect my
bowel, causing me to become emaciated. I couldn't conduct High
Holy Day Services that year. I remember sitting in the congregation at
Yizkor time, and as I heard the names of the deceased being read, I
thought to myself, maybe next year they'll be reading my name.

The spleenectomy had put me into a brief period of remission, but
my condition deteriorated. They tried some kind of experimental
chemotherapy, but to no avail. My health further deteriorated. It
turned out that, in addition to hairy cell leukemia, I had contracted a
rare form of tuberculosis that afflicts people with AIDS. About 95%
of my bone marrow was malignant and I was dying of tuberculosis.

Fighting for my life in the hospital, I was heartened by the news
that in Chicago seven patients with my type of leukemia had
responded well to an experimental dose of the drug interferon. I
prayed that I might be eligible for inclusion in the study. My diagnosis did not fit the parameters of the experiment but one of the doctors

appealed to the FDA for an exception in my case. Following an angel of mercy flight to the University of Chicago Hospital, I learned permission had been granted.

They gave me interferon injections after operating on my lung. I was in a great deal of pain and refused to leave my bed. The doctors shamed me into action by saying, "Rabbi Jaffe, we know you're having difficulty, but there are other people here. Maybe you could minister to them. Why don't you be a rabbi?"

In the physical therapy room I saw a young man in a wheelchair. He had spinal cancer. Grunting and grimacing, he was trying to lift himself from his wheelchair onto parallel bars. The staff was cheering him on: "Come on, Jerry, you can do it." Finally with a great effort he lifted himself up, maybe an eighth of an inch. I thought, boy, that young man really has guts. Remembering what the doctors said—that I needed to get out of myself and minister to other people—I decided to go see Jerry that night.

I wheeled myself into his room and saw him lying in bed shivering with fever. He started the conversation: "How you doing, fella? Did you see your doctors today?" In despair, I replied, "I think they're avoiding me. They don't want to tell me the bad news." "Just a minute, Hirshel," he said, "aren't you a rabbi?" I nodded. "Well," he continued, "I don't know much about your religion, but I heard somewhere that the Jewish people are a people of hope. Why don't you practice what you preach?" His comment stunned me. Here was a young Christian who was more in touch with the yearnings of my Jewish spirit than I. The irony of the encounter brought me to an epiphany, a transformation.

In the next few months the leukemia loosened its grip on me. The fevers and coughing subsided. I was still emaciated but no longer saw myself as crippled. I resolved to get out of the hospital and embark on my God-given mission to give help to people who were suffering.

In the Spring of 1993 my health began to fail. I was treated by a new experimental drug, which my doctors believe has finally conquered the leukemia.

I have since committed my life to counseling people of every faith who face serious illness or other adversity, speaking all over the country and often appearing as a "Celebrity Against Cancer." In March,

1988 President Ronald Reagan presented me with the American Cancer Society's Award of Courage. And for the last three years, I have joined the Leukemia Society Team at the 20-mile marker of the New York Marathon and run the last 6 miles through Central Park to the finish line. I can be identified by my t-shirt—"The Running Rabbi."

TAMARA GREEN

For nearly 30 years I have lived with a debilitating chronic illness, sometimes with detachment, sometimes with an amorphous sense of unease, and sometimes with a great deal of rage. It is not immediately life-threatening, although there have been moments when it has been, but it is life-encompassing; and one of the most painful lessons I have learned from this illness is that what is most difficult to come to terms with is not the possibility of dying from it, but living with it.

Although chronic illness has had the virtue of allowing me to contemplate a great many things, not the least of which is the recognition of my mortality and of the fragility of human existence, what concerns me here are the ways in which my Jewish life has been affected by my illness, and the ways in which my illness has affected my understanding of what it means to be Jewish. Could I find a Jewish understanding of illness that would allow me to live Jewishly with being sick?

One of the first things I discovered were the injunctions concerning the remarkable *mitzvah* of *bikur cholim,* visiting the sick, although the rabbinic discussions focus their attention not on the sick person but on the performance of the *mitzvah* by those who are not sick. As both a frequent recipient and visitor, I learned that it is, in fact, an act of *chesed,* kindness, that is gratifying beyond measure. Judaism, after all, is a religion that ultimately finds its spiritual center in concrete acts: Torah is always telling us what to do. But certain deeds are singled out by the ancient sages as having special importance. According to the Talmud, of all of Adonai's acts of lovingkindness towards the creation that humans can imitate, one of the most important is the act of visiting the sick. It has been traditionally the means by which the community of Israel has performed acts of lovingkindness, a way of acknowledging the suffering of others, and of embracing everyone within the community.

I discovered as well that what traditional Jewish texts had to say about the causes and consequences of illness was too often painful to bear, and even alienating, and I found myself struggling angrily with them all the time. In part, my anger had to do with what I regarded as the harsh and even punitive outlook expressed in the texts. Stories found in Torah and elsewhere that deal with illness, such as those of Abraham, Miriam, and even Job, are predicated on the belief that Adonai can and will heal them all.

What follows is a brief summary of the various Jewish meanings of illness I uncovered, and my own responses to them. Neither side, I must warn you, is consistent in its understanding.

1. My illness is a punishment from Adonai. If illness is a punishment, what did I do that was so terrible and could I be forgiven?

2. My illness is a way of making me spiritually aware. I can state unequivocally that pain and suffering have done nothing to ennoble me. And since I have not gotten any better, does that mean I haven't learned whatever lesson Adonai wanted to teach me? What happens if pain becomes a way of destroying faith, not strengthening it?

3. Adonai loves the tears (Berachot 32). My only response to that is: what about my tears? Besides, if Adonai is full of compassion, how could Adonai love my tears?

4. Elucidation is beyond the grasp of the human intellect. I would like to give it a shot; after all, I have a PhD. But if I concede that the plans of Adonai for the creation are beyond my comprehension, what hope can I have of making sense of what has happened to me?

5. Adonai controls the world, but not completely. If Adonai created the world, how could it be possible that the Divine Power does not control everything in the creation? But if that is true, how can I turn to Adonai, if Adonai can do nothing about my pain? Or does Adonai just heal some of us, and not others? I would like to believe that Adonai is just and Adonai is omnipo-

tent; but, as more than one theologian has pointed out, one of these assumptions must be false in the face of human suffering.

The texts say we are all created in Adonai's image. Does this mean that Adonai also walks with crutches, has difficulty breathing, and suffers from digestive trouble? We recite in the Selichot service: *Haneshama lach v'haguf paa'lach*—"The soul is Yours, and the body is Your handiwork." How come, then, Adonai did such a lousy job with my body?

If studying the texts seemed only to emphasize my sense of isolation, could I at least find solace in the pleasurable rhythms of a life lived Jewishly? In many ways I could, but periodically the spiritual complications of physical illness overwhelm me. Here are some random memories.

I love going to my synagogue, where we have created a true sense of Jewish community. And yet, even there, I sometimes find myself distressed. I know that it really doesn't matter whether I sit when everyone else stands, but when we sing *L'cha Dodi* on Friday night, it is only with great difficulty that I can rise with the rest of the congregation to welcome the Shabbat Bride.

From the time I learned the words as a child, my favorite Shabbat song has been *Adon Olam*, but on one Shabbat I felt my eyes fill with tears as I sang the words *v'hu Eli v'chai goali, v'tsur chevli b'es tsara,* "He is my God and my life's redeemer, my refuge in distress." How could I sing these words when I felt that they had nothing to do with me?

One Shabbat morning, when the physical pain was particularly bad, I wondered whether I could recite a *Mi Sheberach,* a prayer of healing, for myself.

While preparing for Pesach one year, I was struck by the notion that my illness was like *chamets* that no amount of cleaning could get rid of. At the seder I resented the fact that unlike the ancient Israelites, I would never be liberated from my burden. As I dipped my finger in the wine to count off the ten plagues, I suddenly felt as if they had been sent by Adonai not against the Egyptians, but against me.

It took me a long time and a lot of struggling before it finally struck me that I had been asking the wrong questions. The questions I really needed to ask were: could I be spiritually healed even if I never got any better physically; and if I was not to be cured, what did Adonai expect of me?

Since I am an academic, perhaps it is not surprising that the paths I explored, once I knew what questions to ask, were through texts. I discovered a talmudic and a kabbalistic text that provoked in me healing images of enormous power.

The first, from the Talmud, has as its starting point the episode of the Golden Calf. Torah says that when Moses descended from Mt. Sinai with the tablets of law and found the people worshiping the Golden Calf, he smashed the tablets in anger. Although he returned to the mountain to receive new tablets, the broken shards were not discarded; they were preserved and placed in the Ark along with the second set, to be carried by the Israelites everywhere, even into the Promised Land. Both the shattered tablets and the whole ones were together in the Ark of the Covenant. There must have been at Sinai some children of Israel who, like me, were physically broken; who saw themselves, as I did, in those fragments of the tablets; and who, like me, were relieved to find themselves included in the Covenant.

That provided an answer to my first question, but the second— what does Adonai want of me?—was more difficult. An approach came from an unexpected source: Jewish mystical teachings. The 16th-century kabbalist Rabbi Isaac Luria declared the spiritual world was the product of emanations that flowed from a transcendent God, who could be known only through these ten emanations (wisdom, justice and the like) that were contained in vessels. But their divine light was too powerful to be contained, and all but three vessels shattered as Adonai contracted to make room for the creation of the physical world, thus allowing the spiritual to mix with the material world. As a result, these divine emanations, most notably the *Shechinah*, the Divine Presence, are in exile in this world, the vessels that once held them now broken. And these divine sparks of light, trapped in matter, must be released from their prison; for only with the restoration of the spiritual world to its original completeness will redemption of Adonai's creation be possible.

It seems like an impossible task, but Rabbi Luria revealed the way to bring about *tikun olam,* the repair of the world: every person who acts in accordance with Torah brings home the fallen sparks; everywhere in the world a spark of the Divine Presence is waiting to be found, gathered and restored, and Adonai holds out the possibility to each generation that it might be the one to redeem the world. Each one of us, then, has the potential to bring about *tikun olam,* not only through the performance of the commandments but through acts of *chesed,* lovingkindness.

The shattered tablets in the Ark of the Covenant have helped me to see that I don't have to be physically whole to be part of the community of Israel. And I have come to realize that spiritual repair, both of myself and the world, is possible. I may not be able to do much about the broken vessel that is my body, but I can help to gather up the scattered light.

Our Power to Touch and Heal

DEBBIE FRIEDMAN

When I moved to New York, my first apartment was next door to a synagogue. I moved to this apartment in September, just before the High Holy Days. For the first time in my life not only did I not have to worry about the distance to *shul*, I didn't even have to worry about parking.

The davening on Rosh HaShanah was a beautiful experience. The whole congregation was elevated as we sang the prayers together in a variety of *niggunim* that were superimposed on the liturgy. I was sorry when the second day was over. I could have stayed there forever, immersed in song and prayer.

Then came the day of *Kol Nidrei*. *Kol Nidrei*: I used to think *Kol Nidrei* was a prayer but learned it was actually a declaration. The whole ritual of *Kol Nidrei* was a reenactment of going to court. We declare to God, in the presence of the *sifrei Torah* as witnesses, that before entering into the Yom Kippur spirit of prayer asking for repentance and atonement, we acknowledge that we will make promises we will not keep. We ask that we be absolved of responsibility for any promises made and forgotten, or simply not fulfilled. For so many years I had been the one to sing these words. This *Kol Nidrei* night I looked forward to having the great joy of being one of the congregation.

To my great dismay, early that afternoon I realized I had a fever and would not be able to attend services. I was completely frustrated. I paced around the house with Farfel, my dog, following behind me. Finally, the time came for me to light my *yahrzeit* candles. There were quite a few. I light them for all my family members who are no longer living. I placed the candles on the kitchen counter. Farfel stood by my side as she does when I light Shabbat candles, waiting for her blessing. There was nothing but quiet and the memory of those who were once a part of our family. We also lit a candle for those who had no family, no loved ones, no one to remember them.

Suddenly I heard what I thought was Farfel's collar jingling. The noise continued even though Farfel was still. Something made me look out my kitchen window, but the view was obstructed. I couldn't see much, although I could see a building that resembled the synagogue. Until that moment, I hadn't made the connection between the synagogue next door and the building in the back of my apartment. I quickly realized though that the sanctuary of the synagogue backed up to the alley. And the alley backed up to my family room.

I found my way into the family room. The piano was tucked away in the alcove of the room. The window in the alcove looked out onto the alley. I climbed under the piano with Farfel and we sat down. What I hadn't realized was that I would hear the voice of the community from the sanctuary of my home. The jingling that I had heard, and the quiet that accompanied the jingling, was the congregation removing the *sifrei Torah* from the ark in preparation for the chanting of *Kol Nidrei*.

I looked out the window, and I saw the sanctuary and a sea of *tallitot*. There were no heads, no legs . . . I could only see from necks to waists. Suddenly the rabbi began to sing, chanting alone the first of the three repetitions of *Kol Nidrei. Kol Nidrei* . . . I could hear him sing . . . may I not be held responsible. . . . The second time there were a few voices humming along, and the third time, . . . please absolve me from any responsibility. . . . The voices swelled, filling not only the sanctuary, but the alley as well. Every note was sung, and the sounds of the many voices echoed their way through the alley into my window. Every word . . . every word was crystal clear.

After a while I went to lie down. When I came back, the congregation had just begun to sing *Avinu Malkeinu*. I could not believe that it was at that exact moment I had awakened and returned to my seat at my "piano *shul*." I was completely overwhelmed with the sounds that were coming from the sanctuary. Farfel and I sat there for the rest of the service.

Over 1,000 people were in the synagogue next door that *Kol Nidrei* night. I'm sure that those who attended had no earthly idea of their heavenly powers and how in that short time they gave voice to prayer that transformed the human spirit from a place of pain and despair to one of comfort and healing. How could I possibly thank them? How could they ever know know what a gift they had given to me?

When I moved here, people warned me about New York and New Yorkers. They said it was a rough, hard city and that people were tough. They said it was an unforgiving city. What I wasn't told was that it was a city with many angels, most of whom are completely unaware of their goodness.

We wander through our lives bumbling around, often thinking that we have no power to effect change and that we don't carry much weight in the grand scheme of things. Those of us involved in synagogue life hear much about the ambiguity of our prayer lives. We wonder about the efficacy of our prayers. Some of us ask, "Why bother? Prayer doesn't change my situation. I am still stuck here in this same mess."

Many people are embarrassed or, at best, tentative about having conversations about God. Yet what I attempt to communicate in my work is that God is present in our every breath. It has been my experience that many in search of spirituality look outside of themselves in an attempt to find meaningful ways in which to connect to the community and to God. They are looking for a way to be a part of something larger and at the same time finding a way to explore something more deeply inside of themselves.

There are those moments in our lives when we find ourselves questioning our worth and significance in this world. There are times when we struggle to find our place, wondering for what purpose the Holy One has brought us here. What I learned from my *Kol Nidrei* experience that year in New York is that no matter where we are and no matter what we are doing, our actions are not without reactions. We have the power to touch and to heal people around us, whether at home or on the street, in a service or hospital, or even on the floor under a piano, anywhere at all, simply by being present and allowing ourselves to be our most human and loving selves.

I walk by that *shul* every day, and I see the congregants, and I often wonder: was it you wrapped in the *tallit,* uttering the words of prayer in that sanctuary, or you who sang those prayers that floated all the way back through my window, under the piano, and into my heart? It could have been you. It could be you now. It could be you receiving these prayers now, right here on the street in a look, or a word, or an intention of loving-kindness.

We can never know what happens to the prayers we utter. We do not know what happens to the words we speak with one another. The words we pray might feel useless, and we may feel that they simply dissipate into thin air, gone forever. Once we let them go, they are airborne, out of our control. It is the same with every step and every breath and every movement we make. But we never know. They may be the very thing that is life-giving and healing to another person.

How I Spent My Summer Vacation

DEBBIE PERLMAN *z"l*

Uncertainty
Unspooling duality tangles me
Again and again, my heel catching
In the hem of life's garment,
Stretched long with falling tears.

I seek You in the after glimmer,
After this day's rain of terrible scenes,
New unfolding schemes, new secrets.
You come to calm me, Holy One, with cool light.

You are there with savory goals,
Laid out like a picnic on new grass
To spark an appetite grown weary and becalmed,
Negligent of soul's refreshment.

I think, Holy One, You do not tease
With these delicacies, but rather spread them
For my ease. Giving me breathing space
For another day's maneuvers.

Two weeks before Tisha B'Av, my summer cold accelerated to pneumonia, my maneuvers became a day-by-day struggle toward recovery. My breathing space was counted and quantified by physicians and nurses and respiratory therapists. And by family and friends, an entire congregation that sent their own energies of healing and caring for my consumption.

I have been disabled and oxygen dependent for a long time. The result of radiation and chemotherapy for Hodgkin's disease, a form of cancer, that spared my life in my twenties and thirties, I face the realities of these aftereffects with thanks that I am alive. For me, pneumonia was a challenge handled poorly by my body. When I woke up several days later in the intensive care unit, I found that the days lost to me had been busy for my caretakers.

Intensive Care Unit
Hooked, Holy One, linked and lined,
To openings divine and necessary;
Hooked, Divine Healer, to computer pads, data recorders,
Divining and rejoining every breath and beat.

Hooked to kind friends arriving,
Who bring Shabbat with electric bulbs,
Their voices joining as I weep,
Linked to lines, to them, to You.

Hooked, as choking, terrified,
Calm nurse hands move efficiently,
Setting aright, clearing, relieving,
Aligning me toward recovery.

I am hooked, Divine One.
I am hooked to this medicine and mystery,
To the human hands in Your stead,
Guarding and rehearsing my complete healing.

Earlier in the year, I had been named "Psalmist in Residence" of my congregation, Beth Emet The Free Synagogue in Evanston, Illinois. My psalms are included in our monthly Healing Service, during Shabbat and holiday worship, and for events in the life cycle of the congregation. Their effect has been startling and humbling. I found that my voice was able to speak for people as superficially disparate as a nun doing parish work and a Lubavitcher mother of five who is also a computer specialist. After publishing my first book, *Psalms for a New Day,* in 1995, I began to receive comments from people who kept my book in their nightstands, who turned to my verses to ease their lives.

In the hospital, as I found myself fighting pain and confusion, I was drawn again and again to remember a recently assimilated piece of text: the last stanza of David's Psalm 150.

Praise God with resounding cymbals!
Praise God with clanging cymbals!
Let every soul that has breath praise God!
Hallelujah!

Earlier in the summer, I had read *Healing of Mind, Healing of Body* (Rabbi Simkha Y. Weintraub, ed. [Woodstock, Vt.: Jewish Lights Publishing, 1994]). Finally the idea of "all my soul" became real. The festival melody for the psalm played in my head as I was wheeled to a special procedures room to have a tracheostomy performed. It would return often as I became more alert and more able to move around, its cadences helping me to regulate my breathing as I exercised.

Intensive Care Unit II
My heart calls You, Holy One,
My heart bottom, bone marrow,
Flesh of soul of being,
Calls You to my questioning.

My heart calls in the suddenness
Of my distress, and the mute days
When I praise forgetting
And compliance, choice surrendered,

My heart calls You in the wakeful times,
Surfacing, succumbing. You are there,
Sustaining my momentary consciousness,
Reminding me to praise You in this place.

Ancient words remind me. Newly learned,
I clutch them tightly, syllable and tone.
You hover in their echo, Holy One,
Supporting my courage and my hope.

I was discharged home only to be readmitted less than two weeks later. The same scenario: more fluid in my chest, more clogged bronchi, more pneumonia. Then another period of lost days, as sedated and mute, I tried to communicate through rapidly scribbled notes. It is difficult to carry on conversations like this; it's impossible to kibitz, to joke, to schmooze. Despite my improving skill at mouthing words and mimicry, the frustration of being misunderstood grew. And the terror of this second contest, a second struggle over the increasingly familiar terrain of intensive care unit and ventilators, triple lumen lines and catheters, shook my faith. It was Elul. It was the time of reflection and preparation for the Days of Awe. And I was still fighting to breathe on my own.

Search for Recovery
Gasping beneath this waterfall of illness,
Frozen limbs straining,
Lungs pushing against the crash,
Heart crying out in rapid beat.

Gasping, Sacred Healer, frantic
To whisper Your name,
To grasp blessing and power
And raise it in shelter.

Torrents overwhelm me,
Drown me in foaming water.
My hand moves, reaching, rising
To protect my face.

Turn to me, Holy One!
Turn back the blasting water,
The pain and sadness,
The shuddering of chances lost.

Turn to me, Sacred Healer!
Multiply my tiny motions
To bring my passage
To dry land.

Home again, I was physically stronger, walking farther. But not able to maintain the recovery, I was admitted again on the afternoon of Erev Rosh HaShanah. Weeping and frightened, a chest tube was inserted to drain the reaccummulated fluid. The next day, I was able to hear the Morning Service over the telephone, through concerted and loving effort by my synagogue's staff. But on the second day of Rosh HaShanah, I crashed. Back to the ICU, to the waking sleep that would leave no memories, to muteness and terror and total dependence.

Months before, I had accepted the honor of creating a psalm that I would read to open the *Kol Nidrei* service. I knew I would not be there to read it. But I knew I had to create something new to defy the reality of these weeks of illness.

Kol Nidrei
Ruler of the universe!
At our season of renewal,
We are turning, bending,
Viewing front and back.

Ruler of the universe!
At our season of revival,
We are uncovering, revealing,
Sweeping out.

Ruler of blessing,
We lean upon the Gate,
Testing the hinges,
Rubbing sharp edges.

Ruler of mercy,
We test our souls,
Rubbing fresh cloth over sorrow,
Binding away disappointment.

Called, called to the Gate,
We jostle, then quiet,
As memory and hope
Soothe us.

Standing, striving,
We empty our hearts' longing
Before You, Holy One,
Source of life.

I did not hear my psalm read. The synagogue's impenitent sound system refused to cooperate. But I knew it had been read. The next day, as friends stopped by before the Afternoon Service, they brought me news of its reception.

I could not break a fast I had not observed. The Ten Days had moved me from a regular floor to the intensive care unit and, on the afternoon of Yom Kippur, back to my regular room. Everyone was familiar by now. I was greeted with kindness and dismay as once again I went through the process of shedding I.V. lines and other tubes and moving from assisted to independent breathing. I regained my voice through the miracle of a one-way valve that lets air in but directs it out past the vocal chords. The gaping hole of the tracheostomy was allowed to become smaller. Physical therapy resumed.

All these days incarcerated! For the first time in many years, we did not build our sukkah. But on the Sunday in Sukkot, a young couple bearing *lulav* and *etrog* to hospitalized Jews gave me back a piece of that holiness as I stood by the bed in my purple robe and shook the four species in all directions.

The doctors planned my discharge for the afternoon of Simchat Torah. I had fantasies of attending Beth Emet's celebration. I was released two days later.

Home Again
Strengthen me, Holy One, on my walk from illness,
Even as You gave courage
As the children fled from Egypt;
Open the sea to my steps.

Like a Hebrew slave,
I have sojourned in pain;
Under whips of illness and despair,
I have shed my tears of bitterness.

Show me again the path of freedom,
Speeding toward a Promised Land
Of wholeness and health,
Creating my completeness for Your sake.

Bring me up through recovery,
Through remedies and therapies,
To an altered yet acceptable life,
Again rejoicing in the commonplace.

Then will my songs fill this recovered shore,
Where my mind will dance for joy
At my deliverance,
Singing Your praises, Holy One, singing new songs.

Passage to Wholeness

RABBI ERIC WEISS

Being sick is like being a stranger to one's own life. We feel it most acutely in our intimate circles. With illness comes profound changes in our relationships. Loved ones must consider our needs in a different way. Friendships must adjust to survive. It is a time in which we need to draw upon our spiritual and religious will, regardless of how much or how little we used it in the past. It is a time to deepen our connection with our Jewish souls.

When Margalit first called me, she had been recently diagnosed with cancer. Her mother had suffered from this same form of the disease and died of it at an early age, when Margalit was only fourteen. Unlike her mother, however, Margalit had resources to draw upon at this overwhelming time in her life. From her many years of being involved in the Jewish community, Margalit knew where to seek the kind of spiritual healing she needed more than anything.

Margalit came to me for help. What concrete steps could she take to find meaning through this crisis?

We settled into comfortable chairs in my office, a quiet space far away from screeching horns and ringing phones. I asked Margalit what gave her a sense of awe.

"When I'm doing things with my family," she replied. "It's just amazing to me that I have this wonderful husband who loves and supports me, and a daughter I once dreamed of having who's now a wonderful young woman. It's a blessing."

As she spoke, she realized that being with her family was helping her to overcome fear about the future. "With them I somehow don't feel so afraid of all the medical treatments," she said, an uplift in her voice.

We both smiled. "Let me tell you two Jewish stories," I said, "which offer some spiritual wisdom about the power of relationships to heal us. Centuries ago, in Jerusalem, there lived a man known as Honi the circle-maker, who was renowned for the way he prayed for rain. As the people gathered around him, he would slowly draw a circle and step inside it. There, he would pray for rain. And, miraculously, rain fell." "My family and friends have circled around me, too," said Margalit. "I just never thought of it as something I could connect to Jewish tradition." Margalit then seized on an idea: she could form circles of caring with the support of her family and friends. "I can use Honi as a guide to pay attention to what I need and how people can help me."

"The second story," I went on, "is from Torah. In Exodus we read that Jethro brings his grandsons, Gershom and Eliezer, back to their father Moses after God has saved the Israelites. Gershom is commonly translated as 'I was a stranger there' and Eliezer as 'My God will help.'" "The biblical names," Margalit said excitedly, "are just like my own family, making the journey from being a Gershom to an Eliezer! I understand how harsh it's been for them when I became ill. I'm not my old self, and I can't be there for them in the ways they've grown accustomed to, so they feel like they're in a foreign place, too." Linking Jethro's family and her own, she announced: "I'm taking my family with me on my healing journey."

The chemotherapy Margalit underwent was harsh. She wondered where God was while she was in her bed watching the clear fluid enter into her veins. Margalit assumed that God did not enter hospitals, and this intensified her sense of estrangement. I suggested she use her imagination and sense of wonder to bring God into the room. "How would you feel if there was a *mezuzah* on the door of the hospital room?" I asked her. "Oh, it would be great," she smiled. I explained that in ancient times a *mezuzah* was actually a door frame. The words of the *Shema*—"Hear, O Israel, Adonai is our God, Adonai is One"— contained in the *mezuzah* today were once written on the door frame itself.

"What if the room itself became a *mezuzah*?" I asked. "Then the hospital room would be a holy place where God listened," Margalit replied.

Margalit invited God into the hospital room. Though the chemotherapy was no less severe on her body, her sense of God's presence reduced her anxiety. When our conversation ended, she wanted to recognize her new perception with a blessing. And so began a tradition of reciting a spontaneous prayer that suited the moment, and it always concluded with the priestly benediction: "May God bless you and protect you always. May God's face shine upon you and may this light and warmth be gracious to you. May God's face be ever lifted up toward you, and may this Divine regard for you, this holy attention, bring you the most precious of all sacred gifts: peace, wholeness, *shalom*."

When the chemotherapy treatment cycle ended, Margalit wanted to bring her circle of caring to a ritual of thanksgiving that recognized this transition. "But what kind of ritual?" she wondered. We thought back to the many questions she had posed about God's presence during the course of treatment: "Is God only in Heaven?" "Is God with us on Earth?" "Is God in both places?" "Where do I fit in God's creation?" We reread the creation story for insight. "One interesting aspect of the story," I commented, "is the omnipresence of water. Water is the only element of Creation that exists in Heaven, on Earth, and within the human body. It is as if water represents that God is everywhere."

"I once went to a *mikveh* [ritual bath] with a friend. It was so powerful. That's it—that's what I want to do now." Margalit decided to create a circle of caring ritual with her closest women friends at the local *mikveh*.

"*Baruch ata Adonai*. Blessed are You, Adonai our God, Sovereign of the universe, whose nurturance of us as we travel through life has brought us to this particular time and place." Margalit and her female friends recited this blessing as they immersed themselves in the living waters of the ritual bath. In the currents Margalit expressed her gratefulness for life, her thankfulness to all the loved ones who had shlepped her to doctors' offices, helped with errands, sent cards, left supportive messages on her answering machine, and prayed for her in so many ways. She sang songs, recited prayers, laughed, and cried as she immersed herself in the water, acknowledging all that was sacred to her about life. After each dip and each prayer, her friends uttered "*amen.*" This acknowledgment of God's abiding presence and the enduring love of friendship prepared Margalit for her next medical challenge.

Radiation therapy is among the most isolating of medical treatments. A door closes and the patient is left alone beneath a machine which delivers powerful bolts of radiation to her body. During those moments, Margalit felt painfully disconnected, shut out of her circle of caring. We found a solution: Margalit would count the *omer* of her radiation, just as Jews traditionally counted the *omer* (a sheaf of barley) of the barley harvest from Passover to Shavuot. Counting the days to its harvest was a way our ancestors contained the anxiety of waiting for what they hoped would be a bounty of food, i.e. a good outcome. Each time Margalit went to the doctor's office for her radiation treatment she would say: "This is the fourth day of the second week of radiation," and then recite, "*Shema Yisrael Adonai Eloheynu Adonai Echad.* Hear O Israel, Adonai is our God, Adonai is One." She would allow her inner thoughts to surface, then sit down in a corner of the doctor's office and record the experience in her journal.

At the end of Margalit's radiation cycle we read the journal. Her reflections had helped define her path to an ever deepening relationship to God and her loved ones. Her writing had also led to some important life decisions. In this way, Margalit's journal had brought her to her own Shavuot, the day Jews celebrate the receiving of the Torah.

There is a story that is told of Rabbi Zusya, who was lying on his deathbed. His disciples said to him: "Rabbi, when you enter Heaven, God will greet you and say that you were as great a teacher as was Moses." Zusya replied, "When I get to Heaven, God will not ask me why I was not more like Moses. God will ask me why I was not more like Zusya."

Toward the end of her life, Margalit came to appreciate this *midrash* (rabbinic legend). She utilized Jewish tools to achieve her own wholeness, created a unique universe for her personal healing, and lived as fully as only *she* could.

The vastness of our tradition allows that what works for one may not work for another. For Margalit, it was Torah, the foundation upon which our tradition is built, that opened her spiritual world. It was as if she truly embodied the words we say during Shabbat as we return the Torah to its ark: "*kol netivotecha shalom:* all journeys that begin with Torah lead to wholeness."

The Fabric of Life

RABBI JULIE SPITZER z"l

I didn't think that God caused my cancer, or that God was going to reach out, somehow, and turn off those replicating, diseased cells.

I became a rabbi 14 years ago because I wanted to help others experience the richness of Jewish life. . . . I served as a congregational rabbi for seven years, and in that time I met with many families who were dealing with the shock of bad medical news. I made countless visits to the dying, saw a few miraculous recoveries and buried far too many. But during that time, even as I empathized, I left all the pain behind at the end of the day and went home to my healthy, safe world—to a loving partner, to my friends, a few cats and a supportive family. Now it was my pain, my world that was turned upside down.

Suddenly, the distinction between clergy and congregant seemed to matter very little. Of course, my training gave me easier access to the healing words of my tradition—Moses' brief but poignant cry for God to heal his sister, Miriam, "O God, pray heal her," or the words of the Psalms. . . . These words have been so comforting to so many. But I didn't have a lock on them: A knowledgeable Jew knows them; a curious layperson can seek them out. . . . Over the years I have shared all of these words and prayers with people in need. Would they bring solace to me now? . . .

I find quite compelling Martin Buber's notion of God being present in the I-Thou . . . those intense moments of relationship when you know you've truly connected with another human being. . . . In those first few weeks after my diagnosis, I drew strength from every card, call, flower and friendly face. I saw each one as a prayer for my well-being. . . . Now [that] I have been living with cancer for more than a year . . . I am much more aware of how, both as a rabbi and a friend, I comfort others who are ill. I hope I never say to anyone, "I know that you will soon be all better." These days, I am more likely to say "I hope things will go as well as possible," or "May you draw strength from as many places as possible in your time of need." Sometimes, I find that words are less important than simply being present—a concept institutionalized relatively early in Jewish history in the commandment to visit the sick. (Indeed, the Sages believed a visit to a sick person took away one-sixtieth of her illness.)

Particularly, I am grateful that Judaism, like so many religions, offers a sacred framework for the ordinary and the extraordinary, even if I haven't yet felt ready to offer the blessing for the safe conclusion of a difficult illness, *Birkat ha-Gomel*, "To You, Eternal One, I offer my thanksgiving, and glorify Your name. I praise You, Eternal God, Sovereign of the Universe: You bestow great goodness upon me."

What is most clear to me, through all of this, is that I am not alone. I am a part of something far greater than any one illness or any one doctor or any one obstacle that may stand in the way of my healing. I am part of the fabric of life, the essence of Creation, at one with the Creative Source.

III

TRADITIONAL
HEALING
TEXTS

Praying for Ourselves

And the water was spent in the bottle, and she cast the child under one of the shrubs. And she went, and sat down opposite him a good way off, as it were a bowshot; for she said, Let me not see the death of the child. And she sat opposite him, and lifted up her voice, and wept. And God heard the voice of the lad; and the angel of God called to Hagar from heaven, and said to her, What ails you, Hagar? Fear not; for God has heard the voice of the lad where he is. Arise, lift up the lad, and hold him in your hand; for I will make him a great nation. And God opened her eyes, and she saw a well of water; and she went, and filled the bottle with water, and gave the lad to drink. And God was with the lad; and he grew, and lived in the wilderness, and became an archer.

Genesis 21:15–20

AND THE ANGEL OF GOD CALLED TO HAGAR (21:17)—for Abraham's sake; while [GOD HATH HEARD THE VOICE OF THE LAD] WHERE HE IS connotes for his own sake, for a sick person's prayers on his own behalf are more efficacious than those of anyone else.

B'reishit Rabbah 53:14

Choose Life

It is not in the heavens,
That you should say,
"Who among us can go up to the heavens and get it for us? . . . "
Neither is it beyond the sea,
That you should say,
"Who among us can cross to the other side of the sea and get it for
　　us? . . . "
No,
This thing is very close to you,
In your mouth
And in your heart,
To observe it.
See I have set before you this day
Life and death,
Blessing and curse . . . .
Choose life—so that you . . . may live.

Deuteronomy 30:12–15, 19

Offering Thanks for Recovery

A poem by King Hezekiah of Judah when he recovered from the illness he had suffered:

I had thought:
I must depart in the middle of my days;
I have been consigned to the gates of Sheol
For the rest of my years.
I thought, I shall never see Yah,
Yah in the land of the living,
Or ever behold men again
Among those who inhabit the earth.
My dwelling is pulled up and removed from me
Like a tent of shepherds;
My life is rolled up like a web
And cut from the thrum.

Only from daybreak to nightfall
Was I kept whole,
Then it was as though a lion
Were breaking all my bones;
I cried out until morning.
(Only from daybreak to nightfall
Was I kept whole.)
I piped like a swift or a swallow,
I moaned like a dove;
As my eyes, all worn, looked to heaven:
"My Lord, I am in straits;
Be my surety!"

What can I say? He promised me,
And He it is who has wrought it.
All my sleep had fled

Because of the bitterness of my soul.
My Lord, for all that and despite it
My life-breath is revived;
You have restored me to health and revived me.
Truly, it was for my own good
That I had such great bitterness:
You saved my life
From the pit of destruction,
For You have cast behind Your back
All my offenses.
For it is not Sheol that praises You,
Not [the Land of] Death that extols You;
Nor do they who descend into the Pit
Hope for Your grace.
The living, only the living
Can give thanks to You
As I do this day;
Fathers relate to children
Your acts of grace:
"[It has pleased] *Adonai* to deliver us,
That is why we offer up music
All the days of our lives
At the House of *Adonai*."

Isaiah 38:9–20

Hope in God

Those who hope in God
will renew their strength
and soar on wings like eagles.

Isaiah 40:31

Healing through Music

But the spirit of *Adonai* departed from Saul, and an evil spirit from *Adonai* troubled him. And Saul's servants said to him, "Behold now, an evil spirit from God troubles you. Let our lord now command your servants, who are before you, to seek out a man who knows how to play on a lyre; and it shall come to pass, when the evil spirit from God is upon you, that he shall play with his hand, and you shall be well."

And Saul said to his servants, "Provide me now a man who can play well, and bring him to me." Then answered one of the servants, and said, "Behold, I have seen a son of Jesse the Bethlehemite, who knows how to play, and a fine warrior man, and a man of war, and prudent in speech, and a handsome person, and *Adonai* is with him." And Saul sent messengers to Jesse, and said, "Send me David your son, who is with the sheep." And Jesse took an ass laden with bread, and a skin of wine, and a kid, and sent them with David his son to Saul.

And David came to Saul, and stood before him; and he loved him greatly; and he became his armor bearer. And Saul sent to Jesse, saying, "Let David, I beseech you, stand before me; for he has found favor in my sight." And it came to pass, when the evil spirit from God was upon Saul, that David took a lyre, and played with his hand; so Saul was refreshed, and was well, and the evil spirit departed from him.

I Samuel 16:14–23

God and Prayer Are Always
with Us in Our Healing

The Holy One said to the Jews: "I have said to you—when you pray, pray in the synagogue in your city. If you cannot pray in the synagogue, pray in your field. If you cannot pray in your field, pray in your house. And if you cannot pray in your house, pray on your bed. And if you cannot pray on your bed, reflect in your heart."

Midrash, Psalm 4:9

Trust in God

Psalm 20
Translated by Rabbi Simkha Y. Weintraub

1. *For the conductor, a* mizmor/*psalm of David:*

2. May Adonai answer you
     on a day of *tsarah*/distress;
         May the name of the God of Jacob
             keep you safe and secure.

3. May God send you help
     from the *kodesh*/special sanctuary,
         and from Zion
             may God support and sustain you.

4. May God remember and receive
     all your meal offerings;
         and your burnt offerings—
             may God accept them forever, *selah.*

5. May God grant you
     what your heart desires,
         fulfilling all your *etzot*/plans.

6. May we shout for joy, celebrating God's delivering you!
     May we grow and raise banners in God's name!
         May Adonai fulfill your every wish!

7. Now I know that God has saved an anointed one;
     God will answer from the heavenly sanctuary of *kodesh*;
         with mighty deliverance by God's "right arm"!

8. These trust in chariots,
    and those, in horsepower—
        but as for us—
            we call upon the name of Adonai our God.

9. They collapse and fall
    but we rally and rise up, with renewed strength.

10. Adonai, *save*!
    The One Ruler will answer us on the day we call out!

Adonai Is My Light

Psalm 27
Translated by Rabbi Simkha Y. Weintraub

A Psalm of David
1. Adonai is my Light and my Help;
    whom will I fear?
   Adonai is the Strength of my life;
    who can make me afraid?

2. When evil people draw near to devour my flesh—
    it is these foes and enemies who stumble and fall.

3. Even if an army rises up against me,
    my heart will have no fear!
   Even if a whole war besets me,
    I will still feel secure.

4. One thing I ask from Adonai,
    one thing I seek:
        to dwell in Adonai's house all the days of my life,
        to gaze upon the beauty of Adonai
        to explore Adonai's sanctuary.

5. Adonai will shelter me in a Sukkah
    on an evil day;
   Adonai will conceal me in the secret shelter of a tent,
    raise me up safely upon a rock.

6. My head is high above my enemies around me;
    I sacrifice in Adonai's tent, to the blasts of trumpets,
     singing and chanting a hymn to Adonai!

7. Adonai—*sh'ma*/hear my voice when I call!
    Have mercy on me and respond!

8. You seek my heart,
    My heart seeks You—
    I seek Your Presence.

9. Do not hide Your Face from me;
    Do not turn Your servant away in anger!
    You have always been my Help
     so do not abandon me, do not forsake me,
      my God, my Saving One.

10. Even if my father and mother abandoned me,
     Adonai would gather me in.

11. Teach me Your ways, Adonai,
     Guide me on a straight and level path,
      because of my watchful enemies.

12. Do not hand me over to my foes;
     ignore the false witnesses and unjust accursers
      who rise up against me,
       breathing violence!

13. I believe I will yet see Adonai's Goodness
     in the Land of Life.

14. Hope in Adonai!
     Be strong inside, and let your heart be brave!
     Yes, yes, hope in Adonai!

Do Not Forsake Me

Psalm 38
Translated by Rabbi Simkha Y. Weintraub

1. A *Psalm of David*, l'hazkir/*a memorial, to remember:*

2. Adonai, do not rebuke me in Your anger;
   do not chasten me in Your wrath.

3. for Your arrows penetrate deep into me,
   Your hand has come down upon me.

4. There is no unmarred spot in my flesh
   because of Your rage;
   neither is there peace in my bones
   because I have missed the mark.

5. For my iniquities have gone over my head,
   as a heavy burden, too weighty for me.

6. My wounds are rotten, festering,
   because of my foolishness.

7. I cringe, bent, bowed down greatly;
   I go about all day, darkened spirits, overcast,

8. for my loins are filled with burning,
   there is no soundness in my flesh.

9. I am numbed, crushed, sorely oppressed;
   I groan and moan from the heart.

10. Adonai, all my desires and needs are before You;
    my sighing is not hidden from You.

11. My heart is engulfed in grief, my strength fails me;
    as for the light of my eyes, it, too, has gone.

12. My friends and companions stand aloof from my affliction,
    my kinfolk stand far off.

13. Those who seek my life lay snares for me;
    and those who seek to hurt speak craftily,
    meditating and uttering deceit all day.

14. But I am as if deaf—I do not hear;
    I am as a mute person, not opening the mouth.

15. Yes, I have become as one who hears nothing,
    in whose mouth are no rebuttals.

16. For You, Adonai, I hope and wait;
    You will respond, Adonai, my God.

17. I had said, "What if they rejoice over me?
    When my foot slips, they exalt themselves over me?"

18. For I am prone to limp, to suffer;
    my pain is continually before me.

19. I realize and declare my inquity,
    I am full of care and anxiety because of my sin;

20. but my enemies abound with health and life,
    those that hate me without cause, have multiplied.

21. Those who repay evil for good
    denounce me because I pursue that which is good.

22. Do not forsake me, Adonai!
    My God, do not be far from me!

23. Rush to help me,
    my Master, my Redemption!

In My Distress

Psalm 86
Translated by Rabbi Simkha Y. Weintraub

1. *A t'fillah/prayer of David:*
   Tilt, Adonai, Your ear—
   Answer me—
   impoverished and needy am I.

2. Guard my soul, my being—
   for I am *hassid*/loyal-devoted;
   Save Your servant
   —You, my God—
   save this one, who trusts in You.

3. Be gracious to me, my Lord,
   for to You I call
   day in and out.

4. Gladden Your servant's soul
   for to You, my Lord
   I lift up my whole being.

5. For You, my Lord, are good and forgiving,
   with ample *hessed*/lovingkindness
   for those who call to You.

6. Lend Your ear, Adonai,
   to my *t'fillah*/prayer,
   Listen, attend, to
   the voice of my supplications.

7. On the day of my distress
   I call out to You,
      for You answer me.

8. There is none like You
   among the "gods,"
      my Lord,
         nothing like Your works.

9. All the nations
   that You made
      will come to bow low before You,
      my Lord,
         giving *kavod*/glory to Your name.

10. For You are great
    You do wonders
       You,
       God,
          just You, alone.

11. Teach me, Adonai,
    Your ways—
       I will walk in Your truth;
          Pull my heart together
          I live in awe of Your name.

12. I thank/praise You, my Lord, my God,
    with my whole heart,
       I glorify Your name
          eternally.

13. Your *hessed*/lovingkindness is so great toward me,
    You have saved my being
       from *Sh'ol*/the gravest depths down below.

14. *Elohim*/God—
     Willful transgressors
       have risen up against me!
       A company of mighty ones sought my being!
       They did not set You before them!

15. But You, my Lord,
       are a God of compassion and grace,
       Slow to anger
       with bountiful *hessed*/lovingkindness and truth.

16. Turn to me
       Be gracious to me
       Give of Your power to Your servant
         and save the son of Your servant!

17. Give me a sign for good,
       Let my enemies see and be ashamed,
         for You, Adonai,
           helped me
           and comforted me.

Do Not Hide Your Face

Psalm 102
Translated by Rabbi Simkha Y. Weintraub

1. *A prayer for a poor man, who wraps himself up,*
     who, before Adonai, pours out his thoughts, his speech:

2. Adonai, hear my prayer,
     let my cry come to You.

3. Do not hide Your face from me;
    in the day of my distress,
      incline Your ear to me;
    on the day that I call,
      answer me right away.

4. For my days are consumed like smoke,
    My bones dried up as a hearth.

5. Beaten down like grass, and withered, is my heart,
    I forget even to eat my bread.

6. From the sound of my sighing,
    my bones cling to my flesh.

7. Like a pelican of the wilderness,
    I have become—
    like an owl of the wastelands.

8. I thought and thought, and was like a lonely bird, alone on a
    roof.

9. All day long, my enemies taunt and revile me;
    Those who mock me, swear.
10. For I have eaten ashes as bread,
    mixed my drink with tears;

11. because of Your fury, Your wrath,
    You lifted me up and cast me down.

12. My days are like a lengthening shadow,
    and I, like grass, dry up and wither away.

13. But You, Adonai, will be enthroned forever,
    Your memory stretches from generation to generation.

14. You will rise up, have mercy on Zion,
     for it is time to be gracious to her,
        the appointed time has come.

15. For Your servants deeply desired her (Zion's) stones,
     and favored its dust.

16. Nations will fear the Name of Adonai
     and all the kings of the earth, Your glory.

17. Adonai has built up Zion,
     appeared in Divine Glory.

18. Adonai has turned to the prayer of the lonely one
     (the one truly of the desert)
     and has never despised their prayer.

19. This will be written for the generation to come,
     A people created anew will praise *Yah*/God

20. who observed from the heights of God's Sanctuary, above,
     Adonai, from heaven, looked down upon the earth.

21.   to hear the anguished cry of the prisoner,
        to liberate those doomed to die.

22.   to proclaim in Zion the Name of Adonai,
        God's praise in Jerusalem.

23. When peoples gather together,
     kingdoms, to serve Adonai.

24. God weakened my strength along the way, shortened my days.

25. I say, "*Eili*! My God!
            Do not remove me in the midst of my days!"
            You, whose years extend throughout all generations!"

26. You laid the foundations of the earth,
    the heavens are the work of Your hands!

27. They will perish, but You will endure;
    all of them will wear out like a garment;
    and as a garment You will change them, and they
    will vanish.

28. But You are the same, the One,
    Your years do not end.

29. Your servant's children
    will be securely settled,
    and their seed will be established before You.

My Help Comes from God

Psalm 121
A Song of Ascents

I lift my eyes to the mountains,
from where will my help come?

My help comes from the Eternal,
Maker of heaven and earth.

The Eternal will not let your foot give way;
your Guardian will not slumber.

See, the Guardian of Israel
neither slumbers nor sleeps!

The Eternal is your keeper
The Eternal is your shade
upon your right hand.

By day the sun will not strike you,
nor the moon by night.

The Eternal will guard you from all harm,
keeping your soul.

The Eternal shall guard your going out and your coming in,
from this time forth and forever.

Suffering and Joy

Do not despair because of suffering,
For life is suffering.
Suffering and also joy.
When life brings you suffering, hurt.
When life brings you joy, laugh.
Cling to nothing
For all is fleeting.

Mishnah Avot 1:7

How Can We Tell When Prayer Works?

Our Rabbis taught: Once the son of Rabban Gamliel fell ill. He sent two scholars to Rabbi Chanina ben Dosa to ask him to pray for him. When he saw them he went up to an upper chamber and prayed for him. When he came down he said to them: Go, the fever has left him. They said to him: Are you a prophet? He replied: I am neither a prophet nor the son of a prophet, but I learnt this from experience. If my prayer is fluent in my mouth, I know that he is accepted; but if not, I know that he is rejected. They sat down and made a note of the exact moment. When they came to Rabban Gamliel, he said to them: By the Temple service! You have not been a moment too soon or too late, but so it happened: at that very moment the fever left him and he asked for water to drink.

Babylonian Talmud, B'rachot 34b

IV

HEALING PRAYERS,
POEMS, AND
MEDITATIONS

As the darkness lifts . . .

NAOMI LEVY

As the darkness lifts, don't let that moment pass without experiencing its full force. Take a walk, even if it's only around the block. Breathe deeply. Gaze at the trees, listen to the birds, look up at the sky, take in the beauty. Eat your favorite food. Savor every bite with a renewed appetite for living. Grate a lemon and smell its rind. Hug your family, thank your friends for standing by you when you were in pain. Ask forgiveness from those you alienated. Stand before a mirror and stare into your own eyes. See the hope that shines through. Tell yourself how far you have come and acknowledge the strength you never knew you had. Sit in a quiet place and talk to God. Express your full range of emotions. Your anger, frustration, and sadness, as well as your joy, relief, and optimism. Give thanks for the power to endure and carry on, for the new day and its promise, for all the blessings you have taken for granted.

Then brace yourself for the struggles that are yet to come.

Hope

CAROL BACKMAN

There are times when each of us is sick with the world
And life weighs upon us like a heavy boulder
We cannot imagine any good or happy thought
We sink further and deeper into the pit of our despair.

There are times when each of us feels sorely hurt
The very thing we loved the most has been taken away
We feel empty, we feel alone, we are afraid.

There are times when all justice has fled
We have been wronged, cheated, unfairly beaten down
How could life deal such inequities?
Why must our burdens be so severe?

These are moments all human beings share
When their hearts sink and their minds
entertain the worst
Fears assail us all
We tremble and shake at problems facing us

At these times a little voice from within us rouses us
Often waiting until we reach the very brink of despair
It tells us that we can indeed prevail
At first in nothing more than a whisper.

So soft at first that we can hardly hear it
But we listen and we begin to heed
"What's it saying to me?" we mutter
And we bend our ear to catch its faint remarks.

And it tells us what we need to hear
From the tragedy or crisis that we feel
Our bodies are once more released
Our minds are turned to brighter thoughts.

This little voice abiding in each of us is—hope
It is not logical or even reasonable
It is our heart telling our head that we cannot surrender
For to give in to the trials of life is to let them win over us.

From a whisper hope grows slowly
First in a moderate tone and finally to a roar
It supersedes fear, sorrow, and even despair
It gives us the courage to try again.

"Pick yourself up," it demands
"Can't you see that tomorrow has better things in store."
And we begin to believe in ourselves, and we arise
To meet tomorrow a little stronger and more prepared.

"Try again! Try until you succeed," it shouts.
And we forget our failures, our losses and all the blows we were
    dealt
Hope offers us another chance to be what we dream
It insists that life is worthwhile and we are on the winning team.

Hope abides in each of us
Giving us the energy to survive
"Life is very good," it assures us
"Carry on with your work, and you will be blessed."

Courage

ANITA MOISE ROSEFIELD ROSENBERG

Adonai, bless me with courage
    Help me gain strength from You
Life has a way of handing us surprises
    that take an amazing amount of courage to overcome
Create in me a clear and steady focus
    a heart that is filled with the awareness that
    Adonai is with me
        on the sunniest day and in the darkest night
I will be whatever life demands of me
Courage is my knowledge of You.

God, I need to know . . .

NAOMI LEVY

God, I need to know that You are with me; that You hear my cry. I long to feel Your presence not just this day but every day. When I am weak and in pain, I need to know You are beside me. That in itself is often comfort enough. I do not pretend to know Your ways, to know why this world You have created can be so beautiful, so magnificent, and yet so harsh, so ugly, and so full of hate. The lot You have bestowed upon me is a heavy one. I am angry. I want to know why: why the innocent must suffer, why life is so full of grief. There are times when I want to have nothing to do with You. When to think of You brings nothing but confusion and ambivalence. And there are times, like this time, when I seek to return to You, when I feel the emptiness that comes when I am far from You. Watch over me and my loved ones. Forgive me for all that I have not been. Help me to appreciate all that I have, and to realize all that I have to offer. Help me to find my way back to You, so that I may never be alone.

Amen.

Five
A Lullaby for Courage

DEBBIE PERLMAN z"l
z"l: E.F.L.

O Eternal, hold me with gentleness
Through this long night of pain;
Lay Your cool hand upon my body.
As a mother strokes the fevered brow
Of her beloved child,
Give me succor.

O Eternal, clasp me to Your bosom,
And rock me with quiet motion,
To and fro as the seconds pass,
Waiting, waiting for the next relief,
Stretching endlessly toward the dawn.

O Eternal, sing me to calm,
Humming a lullaby my grandmother sang
As she arranged the soup bowl on the tray,
And brought it to me with the warmth of her smile.
Sing me that song to soothe my soul.

O Eternal, guard me through this darkness.
Wrap me in a soft, warm quilt of Your regard
That I might find a paragraph of flickering comfort
To read and remember
Within this long, grim novel.

O Eternal, keep me safe through this night;
And let the morning come to renew me,
To turn me, to heal me,
To find me enfolded in the vigor of Your love.

A Prayer for Prayer

RABBI SHELDON ZIMMERMAN

O my God
My soul's compassion
My heart's precious friend
I turn to You.

I need to close out the noise
To rise above the noise
The noise that interrupts—
The noise that separates—
The noise that isolates.
I need to hear You again.

In the silence of my innermost being,
In the fragments of my yearned-for wholeness,
I hear whispers of Your presence—
Echoes of the past when You were with me
When I felt Your nearness
When together we walked—
When You held me close, embraced me in Your love,
laughed with me in my joy.
I yearn to hear You again.

In Your oneness, I find healing.
In the promise of Your love, I am soothed.
In Your wholeness, I too can become whole again.

Please listen to my call—
    help me find the words
    help me find the strength within
    help me shape my mouth, my voice, my heart

so that I can direct my spirit and find You in prayer
In words only my heart can speak
In songs only my soul can sing
Lifting my eyes and heart to You.

Adonai S'fatai Tiftah—open my lips, precious God,
so that I can speak with You again.

Be Strong and of Good Courage!

AUTHOR UNKNOWN

May the One who blesses all life, bless and heal these people who
struggle against life-threatening illness.

May those afflicted with disease be blessed with faith, courage,
loving and caring.

May they know much support and sustenance from their friends,
their loving companions and their communities.

May they be granted a full and complete healing of body and of
soul.

May those who seek ways of healing through increased medical
knowledge and those who care for the sick daily be blessed
with courage, stamina and communal support.

May all, the sick and the well together be granted courage and
hope. And let us say: Amen.

Bless the Healer

AUTHOR UNKNOWN

I thank You, God, for the skill, care, and concern of the many
about me who have dedicated themselves to health and
healing.

It is they who have had to respond to my calls for help: they who
will be with me through the difficult times ahead.

Grant wisdom, patience and understanding to them.

Bless the work of their hands and their hearts that their labors
may not be in vain.

As Your helpers, may they find the way to restore me and others
to a life renewed.

May I and they feel the comfort of Your presence.

A Prayer for Strength

AUTHOR UNKNOWN

O God, our refuge and strength, and an ever-present help in times
of trouble,
how much I need Your strength and presence in my life right
now.
I feel weak, depressed, anxious, even frightened.
I need help to face these hours and days.

So I claim Your promises
that I can bear whatever comes,
that Your strength will be sufficient, and
that my despair will give way to Your peace that passes all
understanding.

Amen.

As we make our way . . .

NAOMI LEVY

As we make our way through our busy and often lonely days, may our thoughts lead us back to times of smiles and laughter. May our tears and pain be eased by the comfort of our memory. And may God offer us strength and comfort now and always.

Amen.

Open Us to Healing

AUTHOR UNKNOWN

There are moments when wellness escapes us, moments when
pain and suffering are not dim possibilities, but all too
agonizing realities. At such moments we must open ourselves
to healing.

Much we can do for ourselves: and what we can do we must
do—healing, no less than illness, is participatory.

But even when we do all we can there is, often, still much left to
be done. And so we turn to our healers, seeking their skill to
aid in our struggle for wellness.
But even when they do all they can do there is, often, still much
left to be done. And so we turn to Life, to the vast Power of
Being that animates the universe as the ocean animates the
wave, seeking to let go of that which blocks our healing.
May those whose lives are gripped in the palm of suffering open,
even now, to the Wonder of Life. May they let go of the hurt
and meet the True Self beyond pain, the Uncarved Block that
is our joyous Unity with Holiness.

A person reaches in three directions:
inward to oneself
up, to God
out to others.

The miracle of life is that
in truly reaching in any one
direction one embraces all three.

Healing

AUTHOR UNKNOWN

Give ear, O Eternal, to my prayer,
heed my plea for mercy.
In my time of trouble I call you,
for You will answer me.

When pain and fatigue are my companions,
Let there be room in my heart for strength.

When days and nights are filled with darkness,
Let the light of courage find its place.

Help me to endure the suffering and dissolve the fear,
Renew within me the calm spirit of trust and peace.

I am hurting, God . . .

NAOMI LEVY

I am hurting, God. I feel lost, helpless, and alone. My tragedy seems so senseless. Help me, God, to embrace what I cannot understand, to find meaning in my suffering. Remind me that though I am powerless to choose my fate, I hold the power to choose a response to my fate. May I never be defeated. May I never grow bitter. May my sorrow lead me to strength, to wisdom, to compassion, and to You.

Amen.

I ask God for health . . .

AUTHOR UNKNOWN

I ask God for health that I might do great things.
I was given infirmity that I might do better things.
I asked for strength that I might lead,
I was given weakness that I might learn humbly to obey.
I asked for riches that I might be happy,
I was given poverty so that I might be wise.
I asked for power that I might have the praise of people,
I was given weakness that I might feel the need of God.
I asked for all things that I might enjoy life,
I was given life that I might enjoy all things.
I got nothing that I asked for,
but everything that I hoped for.
Almost despite myself,
my unspoken prayers were answered.
I am among all people most richly blessed.

Nine

For Complete Healing

DEBBIE PERLMAN *z"l*
z"l: C.R.S.

Like a pure crystalline tone,
Sounding in the deepest fear of night,
So will You call to me
To leave this land of my distress.

O let me turn to You,
Let me loose the steel bands of my dread
And listen for the ringing
Of Your summons.

How can I leave with so much undone?
How can I move away from this place,
And follow, fearless, into the strength
Of Your concern for me?

I am only Your creation,
Striving to create my own remembrance,
To leave this world with knowledge
Of my passage through it.

So soon You call me to Your harmonies,
To close my manuscript,
To sing unaccompanied
These notes of my life, the final hymns.

Still my terror with clear notes, Righteous One;
Quiet me with a silken melody,
That by accepting Your judgement,
I might turn to sing with You.

Psalm 28

For the Caregivers

DEBBIE PERLMAN *z"l*

Show me how to offer hope.
Open Your hand with the colors of faith
That I might begin to fill in spaces
To strengthen another's life.

Show me how to offer comfort.
Point out Your nesting place,
Feathered against the adversities
That wound those I love.

Show me the direction
When I am lost,
Searching to help
But finding no paths.

Show me tolerance,
When I weary of helping,
And a long dreary day
Stretches toward a restless night.

You place before us life and love;
Show us endurance.
You place before us healing and hope;
Show us persistence.

Reach deep within me, Eternal Strength,
And bring my strength to consciousness.
Pull it around us:
Let it radiate with Your power,
Let it guide our way.

On Recovery

RABBI CHAIM STERN z"l

For health of body and spirit, I thank You, my God. I was broken and now am whole; weary, but now am rested; anxious, but now am reassured.

Teach me to show my thankfulness to all who helped me in my need, who heartened me when I was afraid, and who visited me when I was lonely. For the strength You created within me, O God, I give thanks to You.

Meditation

ANONYMOUS

Source of Healing and Strength
I wonder if anything is impossible for a God
who can make evergreen trees with black trunks
cast blue shadows on white snow.

The world is new to us . . .

BAAL SHEM TOV

The world is new to us
every morning—
that is the Lord's gift
and we should believe
we are reborn each day.

Why does it take a traumatic event . . . ?

ELLEN Y. ROSENBERG

Why does it take a traumatic event,
A moment of crisis
To bring us to our senses,
To shake us up?
Why must we face or learn about illness,
Misfortune, accident or death,
To set our priorities right?
What makes today a special day?
I woke up this morning.
The sun was shining, it was beautiful,
It was dreary, it was raining,
Whatever—it was another day.
I can think,
I can touch,
I can smell,
I can breathe,
I can feel.
I can talk to those I care about
And those who care about me.
I can do whatever I want
That might benefit someone or something.
I can learn,
Expand my interests and my horizons.
How fortunate I am
To be able,
To do and see so much.
Look me straight in the eye
And I will tell you,
Each day is a special day.

God, often I think . . .

JANET CARO MURPHY

God, often I think
You are the only One who listens to me.
That's enough.

Hineini

BARBARA WOLPAW DROSSIN

God called to Moses and Moses cried *"Hineini,* here am I."
Exodus 4:3

I tremble before Thee
Hineini
Weak of will
And frail with age
Worried to live until
I'm done with living

I bow my head before Thee
Hineini
Once I was important
To my loved ones
and my friends
Now I am a nuisance

I beg a question before Thee
Hineini
Has my earthly sojourn
Completed soon enough
Meant anything at all
To You Who lives forever?

I humbly entreat before Thee
Hineini
Love me for all I was
and whatever now remains
the culmination of a life
Spent loving You

My soul opens up before Thee
Hineini
In the endless time to come
allow my caring essence
To flourish yet again
So that my children's children
Will want to bow before Thee
And cry *Hineini*.

Ten

For Healing

DEBBIE PERLMAN *z"l*

Surround me with stillness,
Tiny ripples spreading across the pond,
Touched by one finger of Your hand,
Calmed by the warmth of Your palm.

Croon the wordless melody
That fills my being with peace.

Under the spreading tree of Your affection,
I will sit and meditate
On the goodnesses You have brought,
Counting the happy moments like glistening beads
Strung to adorn my days.

Light the shadowed corners with gentle glow,
To fill my being with peace.

Drape about me the dappled sunlight of Your teachings,
Opening my eyes to the search,
Clearing my heart of small distractions
That I might find the answers within myself.

Blow the breeze of compassion upon my brow,
Breathing the sigh of peace.

Let me rest by the water,
Probing gently for the sense of what I see,
Releasing my hurts to restore my spirit,
Feeling You guide me toward a distant shore.

Mi Sheberach for Shalom Bayit

RABBI RENNI S. ALTMAN

Mi Sheberach avoteinu v'imoteinu,
May the One who blessed our ancestors,
Bless all who involve themselves in the sacred obligation of
  sustaining Judaism.

On this Shabbat, O God, we ask Your blessing
  upon families whose religious backgrounds may differ,
  but who share in the commitment of building a Jewish home—

those who have chosen Judaism as their own
  and those who share in the commitment of a Jewish spouse.

May the shared values of their respective religious backgrounds
  be a source of strength for them, binding them ever closer
  together.

Enable them, O God, to strive for harmony in their homes,
  shalom bayit, during challenging moments when differences
  arise.
Through understanding and mutual respect, may they achieve
  shalom, a sense of wholeness.

And may their loved ones, coming from different religious
  traditions, always feel a part of their home;
May they, too, gain meaning and enrichment from the traditions
  of Judaism that are now a part of the life of their family.

May the blessings of peace, love and happiness reign in their
  homes,
And let us say: Amen.

After a Stillbirth or
Upon the Death of a Young Child

RABBI CHAIM STERN z"l

"Out of the depths I call to You, Eternal One. O God hearken to my voice." (Psalm 130:1–2)

We looked for joy,
and now suddenly,
birds sing,
but not our child.

We looked for life
and now, suddenly,
trees bloom,
but not our child.

How our laughter has turned into grief, our mirth to tears! Hope was full within us; now it is turned to sorrow and lamentation. O God, from You we come, to You we go, You have been our refuge in all generations. Take our grief, and make us whole again, as it is written: "You shall forget your misery, and remember it only as waters that pass away." (Job 11:16)

Upon Terminating a Pregnancy

RABBI DONNA BERMAN

Mother of all life: I need You. I need Your comfort and love; I yearn to rest my head on Your tender breast. Rock me in Your arms as I reflect upon the meanings of life and loss.

Awed by the creative powers within my body, I look back with sadness on the life that could not be. Like a wanderer in a desert I need help: give me shade, quench my thirst. I seek Your warm embrace, that I may drift into healing sleep and arise again, ready to re-enter the garden of Your world.

Prayer after a Miscarriage

RABBI SANDY EISENBERG SASSO

God, we are weary and grieved. We were anticipating the birth of a child, but the promise of life was ended too soon. Our arms yearned to cradle new life, our mouths to sing soft lullabies. Our hearts ache from the emptiness and the silence. We are saddened and we are angry. We weep and we mourn. Weep with us, God, Creator of Life, for the life that could not be.

Source of healing, help us to find healing, among those who care for us and those for whom we care. Shelter us under wings of love and help us to stand up again for life even as we mourn our loss.

Healing after a Miscarriage

MERLE FELD

Nothing helps. I taste ashes
in my mouth. My eyes are flat,
dead. I want no platitudes,
no stupid shallow comfort.
I hate all pregnant women,
all new mothers, all soft babies.

The space I'd made inside myself
where I'd moved over
to give my beloved room to grow—
now there's a tight angry
bitter knot of hatred there instead.

What is my supplication?
Stupid people and new mothers,
leave me alone.
Deliver me, Lord,
of this bitter afterbirth.
Open my heart
to my husband-lover-friend
that we may comfort each other.
Open my womb
that it may yet bear
living fruit.

Divorce is a true passage . . .

RABBI VICKI HOLLANDER

Divorce is a true passage. If we do our work, nothing remains the same. Our traditions are resources, enabling us to break through the numbness; to travel, across the painful transition, safely to the other side. In following the flow and merging into crisis, potential is released for the refining of one's spirit, the stretching of one's soul, the realigning of one's life.

> To what does this compare?
> To the earth
> when it moves and quakes
> and shifts beneath one's feet.
> And when the movement stops
> one walks away shaken,
> touched,
> transformed.

A Song for Comfort before Surgery

DEBBIE PERLMAN *z"l*

Listen!

Because I know You will hear
As I praise You,
As I wonder at this season
That You have brought,
Beginning, even here, to send its
Warmth of renewal over cold earth.

Listen!

Because I know You will hear me
As I fear this unknown I must enter,
Surrendering myself and my mastery,
If only for a little while.

Listen!

Because I know You are there,
Warming me,
Renewing me,
Bringing me through this time
Into a place of health and vigor.

HIV Positive and AIDS

RABBI KAREN BENDER

What can be said of healing to me?
I try to stay healthy and strong, but my diagnosis
and time itself are my enemies.

But I know something that others do not know:
How very precious life is.
The people in my life are very precious.

I pray that every morning when I awake, I will commit
myself to healing and repairing relationships that are important
to me.

I make a difference.

A Special Prayer in Time of Illness

CENTRAL SYNAGOGUE SISTERHOOD

Hear my voice, Adonai, when I call;
Be gracious to and answer me. *(Psalm 27:7)*
In Thy hand is the soul of every living thing,
I turn to Thee, Adonai, in my distress.

Give me patience and faith;
Let not despair overwhelm me.

Renew my trust in Thy mercy
And bless the efforts of all who are helping me.

Be with my dear ones in these difficult days.
Give them strength and courage
To face the anxieties which they share with me.

Grant me Thy healing
So that in vigor of body and mind
I may return to my loved ones
For a life which will be marked by good deeds.

Thou hast ever been my help;
Cast me not off nor forsake me,
O God of my salvation. *(Psalm 27:9)*

My Prayer

MARTY COLEMAN

Thank you God, for You have given me life's treasures of beloved
    family and friends, who have come here to give me their
    healing energy and love through their spirit.

Thank You for allowing me this opportunity.

God, I have prayed for peace for my mind and soul.
I pray for energy and spirit to become whole again.
The pain and sickness my family and I have endured have taught
    us of Your greatness.
I pray that I can be free and whole again.

God, I pray my renewed health gives me the energy to contribute
    to help others who are suffering.

I pray my love and energy reinforces my beloved family and
    friends with health, peace, and knowledge of my gratefulness.

A Patient's Prayer

AUTHOR UNKNOWN

Eternal God, source of healing,
Out of my distress I call upon You.
Help me to sense Your presence
At this difficult time.

You have already sent me gifts of Your goodness:
The skill of my physician,
The concern of others who help me,
The compassion of those I love.

I pray that I may be worthy of all these,
Today and in the days to come.

Help me to banish all bitterness;
Let not despair overcome me.

Grant me patience when the hours are heavy;
Give me courage whenever there is hurt or disappointment.

Keep me trustful in Your love, O God.
Give me strength for today, and hope for tomorrow.

To Your loving hands I commit my spirit—
When asleep and when awake.

You are with me; I shall not fear.
Help me, O God, in my time of need.

The Dew of Life

RABBI NINA BETH CARDIN

Introduction

In Judaism, dew is a restorative elixir graciously dispensed by the hand of God. When the Jews in the desert were desperate for food, God gave them manna, described in Torah as the blossom of dew:

> In the morning there was a layer of dew throughout the camp. And when the layer of dew rose up, behold, a fine delicate substance was on the ground.
>
> Exodus 17:13–14

Dew was the symbol chosen by Isaiah, the prophet who spoke words of comfort to the Jewish people. Spinning visions of times of wholeness, Isaiah [26:19] said:

> For your dew is the dew of light, and with it the land shall bring healing.

The rabbis employ the richness of this symbol in their prayers, creating out of *tal shel ha'aretz*, dew of the earth, the images of *tal shel hayim*, the dew of life, and *tal shel berakhah*, the dew of blessing.

Medicines which drip into our bodies offer the gift of healing. Often, either in the midst of a procedure or in response to our body's reaction afterward, our focus gets diverted from the healing nature of these droplets.

Here we offer a prayer of hope, transforming the stuff of our treatments into *tal shel berakhah*, the dew of blessing.

A prayer to be recited upon receiving chemotherapy (and other intravenous procedures). Adapted from the annual prayer for dew, recited on the first day of Passover, the holiday of our release from bondage.

Kavannah

God, guide my speech and let me give voice to your mysteries.

Prayer *(to be recited when needle is inserted)*

Harahaman, merciful one, open the gates of your wondrous
    storehouse releasing your sparkling dew.

Droplets of life, flow gently, mending the hurt in this body of mine,
    watering the vines of this broken garden.
Droplets of blessing, come gently, fetching a year of goodness,
    filling with peace the reservoir of my soul.
Droplets of dew, heal gently, softening this hard place of blessing,
    giving praise to the work of our Creator.

Droplets of dew,
    come for a blessing and not a curse,
    come for life and not for death,
    come bringing plenty and not emptiness.

A *Yizkor* Meditation in Memory
of a Parent Who Was Hurtful

RABBI BOB SAKS

Dear God,
You know my heart.
Indeed,
You know me better than I know myself,
So I turn to You before I rise for Kaddish.

My emotions swirl as I say this prayer.
The parent I remember was not kind to me.
His/Her death left me with a legacy
of unhealed wounds, of anger and of
dismay that a parent could hurt a child
as I was hurt.

Help me, O God,
To subdue my bitter emotions
That do me no good,
and to find that place in myself
where happier memories may lie hidden,
and where grief for all that could have been,
all that should have been,
may be calmed by forgiveness,
or at least be soothed by the
passage of time.

I pray that You,
who raises up slaves to freedom,
will liberate me from the oppression of my
hurt and anger, and that You will lead me
from this desert to Your holy place.
Amen.

Soften my hardened heart . . .

NAOMI LEVY

Soften my hardened heart, God. In my suffering I have grown callous and unforgiving. Secretly I've been wishing for my friends to fall. But this envy of mine is causing *me* to fall. Teach me, God, to cherish all that I am, all that I have, all that I have yet to offer. Help me to rejoice in the joy of others even when I am in pain; to take pleasure in their pleasure; to wish them nothing but blessings and peace.

Amen.

Blessings and Prayers from
When the Body Hurts,
the Soul Still Longs to Sing

EDITED BY RABBI NANCY FLAM

Mother/Father God, God of the broken-hearted, God of the strong and the weak, God of the angry and the grieving: I stand before You today in pain, in doubt, in fear. Many blessings have been taken from me; I hesitate even to call out to You and yet I must, with every breath, try to speak Your praise, try to be mindful of being alive. O God, thank You for the gift of this breath. Hallelujah.

I thank You God for giving me life today. Please help me to tolerate my pain and that part of my body which is no longer healthy; to love the sick parts and to affirm that which gives me health. By so doing, let me continue to see my own goodness—that which makes me lovable—and to give myself strength and courage to allow my love to touch those in my life whom I love so dearly.

Blessed are You, Source of strength, sustaining Power who has created me and kept me alive with all of the present imperfections of my body.

I awake in pain, misery, and utter confusion; but still I awake. My life is sacred. My life has purpose and my soul houses holy spirit. I pray for healing and to heal others. I gratefully acknowledge today with its infinite possibilities and opportunities. And let me say, Amen.

Blessed is our Eternal God, Creator of the Universe, who has allowed me to experience both great pleasure and the chance to learn of life, for the hope offered by this new day.

Spirit of the Universe, Breath of Life in all forms, with thankfulness I am in Your presence, and You are in me, this body that is failing yet still lives. With You I greet this new day in praise for the wondrousness of all life. Amen.

Thank You God for the light that is breaking through the sky, the sun that shines upon my face, my mind that is still alert and functioning despite my limitations and pain.

Through the day You will join me on this journey, so that I will never be alone or frightened, for I know You will be there. I am thankful for what I am capable of enjoying this day.

Blessed are You, Divine Creator, Mother Earth and Father Sky, my spiritual Parent and Protector. Thank You for giving me another day, another hour, another moment of life.

I hope to find Your comfort and love and grace and courage as I walk through this day.

Blessed is our Eternal God, Creator of the Universe, who has made me as He/She wanted me, so that I may open my heart to love my body/self as I am.

Thank You for opening my heart.

"Blessed is our Eternal God, Creator of the Universe, who has made our bodies in wisdom, combining veins, arteries, and vital organs into a finely balanced network." If any one of those veins, arteries, or organs were to malfunction, I would be reminded of how much I rely on You for my health and well being.

"Wondrous Fashioner and Sustainer of life, Source of our health and our strength, we give You thanks and praise."

Dear God: Thanks for providing me with so many rich experiences and helping lead me down a path woven with loving friends and family. My fond and grateful memories sustain me during this difficult time. I never feel alone with Your guiding presence surrounding me.

The weaker my body becomes, the stronger the fire of my soul burns. Thank You for freeing me from the distractions which prevented me from self-examination and spiritual growth.

Thank You God for giving me all the special, precious things in my life. Please grant me my health and my strength so I can continue to praise You and walk in Your footsteps.

Blessed are You, Eternal God, who has awakened my soul to a new day, allowing me to love and be loved by others.

Portal to Light

NORMA U. LEVITT

A piercing pain in your body
As you wake and cannot turn.
Is this a portal entrance
Into suffering?
Days later in a long tunnel
You move only on demand.
Is there no measure
Of time passing?
No lifting up into lightness
No gathering of will?

Presently thought shines
Through a crystal,
Showing a way to go.
But the lens of words
Remains clogged over.
Is this a portal entrance
Into the isolation
Of never being heard?
Or is it some new quiet
As you bow to move
From the consuming sight
of "I" to a different beat of "us"?

Now on your front door
With a small brush you white out
The name of your life's companion.
Is this only another portal
Into painful remembering?
More than three years later
Is it still a tunnel

In which the nights are long?
Or does time ever passing
Bring healing to every dayness?

Body, mind, spirit . . .
Through the portals of pain.
And the tunnels of suffering,
In time, we stretch and reach
A lifting, struggling upward,
To be again a part of light.

V

RITUALS OF
HEALING

Mastectomy: Twelve Months after Surgery
A Bathing Ritual for the End of Mourning

JERILYN GOODMAN

As the first anniversary of my mastectomy approached, I viewed the occasion with mixed emotions. It had been a year of challenges and discoveries, sadness, fear and fortitude. It had also been, I realized, now that it was over, twelve months of mourning. I had suffered a terrible loss, grieved that loss, and had begun to heal physically and spiritually. It was time to re-enter the world and look towards the future.

I don't remember when the idea of a mikveh immersion ceremony came to me, except that, like so many of the blessings of that year, it came when I both needed it and was open to receiving it.

The healing powers of water had played a big part in my physical recovery from the surgery. Six months before the cancer diagnosis, for reasons I'll never know, I began to swim at the Y. It was an exercise I had attempted a couple of times over the years with no real enthusiasm. Surprisingly, this time I stuck with it and, even more miraculously, began to enjoy it. I built up my strength and endurance and began to feel a sense of peace in the water. It was as if my body knew of the impending trauma and wanted to be prepared. After the surgery (and even now, almost two years later) I continued swimming a few times weekly.

In my mind, a visit to the mikveh offered a ritual cleansing from the ashes of mourning to the freshness of one reborn. It was an appealing thought, but it was only *my* thought, not the *halakhic* idea of our ancestors. Would it, I wondered, be kosher? I consulted my rabbi, Lisa Edwards, at Temple Beth Chayim Chadashim in Los Angeles. She supported me. I had yet no clue, however, as to what my ritual might actually be.

When I was young, our rabbi ended every Shabbat service with the Priestly Blessing. We would rise as a congregation; he would stand in the center of the *bima,* arms raised, and intone this most personal benediction in Hebrew and then in English: "May God bless you and keep you. May God's countenance smile upon you and be gracious unto you. And may God grant you peace. Amen." It was a blessing I could wear as I left the synagogue to face the world outside.

I realized, all these years later, that I wanted the comfort of that same blessing again. It was somehow very embarrassing for me to tell Rabbi Edwards that I wanted to be blessed. But, I reasoned finally, desperate times call for desperate measures. If you can't ask a rabbi to say a prayer on your behalf, whom can you ask?

In the days before going to the mikveh, I started to read up about its significance in *The Jewish Catalog, The Jewish Book of Why, Miriam's Well: Rituals for Jewish Women Around the Year,* and elsewhere. I began reading the Torah, to catch up to the portion for that week (it was Genesis 35:1–36:43). Several passages jumped out at me and I wrote them in a notebook, with no obvious plan.

Besides the rabbi, a dear friend, Fran Chalin, was accompanying me to the mikveh. She had also decided to perform an immersion (in a ceremony completely separate from mine) to celebrate the birth of her first child. Several times we talked about our feelings surrounding the ritual and our expectations. She was particularly fearful that the moment would not instill in her the feelings she wanted to feel.

Hearing her voice these concerns made it easier for me to realize how important it was to let go of expectations. The mikveh would not guarantee me a life free from cancer any more than it would guarantee my friend peace of mind, but if we had no expectations, we could not be disappointed. To enter with an open heart . . . *dayenu.*

The night before my visit, still unsure of what I would do at the mikveh, I sat at the computer consolidating the biblical passages that had struck me. I copied the prayers—the *Sh'ma,* the blessing concerning immersion in the mikveh, and the *Shehechiyanu.* This last prayer especially, thanking God for "allowing us to reach this day," would have particular significance as I stood in the healing waters.

I copied a brief explanation of the states of *tumah* [uncleanliness] and *taharah* [cleanliness] that exist before and after immersion. And suddenly all these passages and prayers fell into an order that would become a service.

At the mikveh the next day, I handed everyone a copy of my ceremony, and then showered and cleaned myself according to custom. Without jewelry, contact lenses, perfumes or anything that would impede the contact of my body with water, I entered the small tile-lined mikveh-room in a towel, disrobed, and went down into the water.

It was a sunken tub, about five feet square, much like any Jacuzzi at a health club, but without the jets. I walked down seven steps to stand in the shoulder-high water. The water was warm and the room quiet. Standing above me were four people—the rabbi; the "mikveh lady" Lillian Zelcer (I had invited her to participate as the "woman who cares for all women"); my friend Fran; and her newborn, Eli. It felt unexpectedly life-affirming to have Eli there.

I stood, arms outstretched and legs apart, as Lillian had instructed me. Each of the three times I immersed, I curled up so that the water enveloped me completely, as it once did in the womb.

Before and after each immersion I relaxed and breathed deeply and let the water and the words of the Torah wash over me, acknowledging my struggle, welcoming God's presence, and preparing me to face the future with hope.

When it was all over, I walked outside into a magnificent late-fall day. The sky felt very close (we were on a hill), very blue. The air was really clean. It felt good and it felt right.

Mikveh Ceremony

Jerilyn Goodman
Los Angeles, November 17, 1994
[To commemorate my mastectomy of November 18, 1993, to mark the end of a year of mourning, and to celebrate my life ahead.]

RABBI: *Tumah* [uncleanliness] is the result of our confrontation with the fact of our own mortality. It is the going down into darkness.

Taharah [cleanliness] is the result of our re-affirmation of our own mortality. It is the re-entry into light. *Tumah* is evil or frightening only when there is no further life. Otherwise, *tumah* is simply part of the human cycle.

[from The Jewish Catalog*]*

RABBI: Be strong and of good courage. Fear not nor be afraid. For the Lord, thy God, will not fail thee nor forsake thee.

[Joshua 1:19]

FRAN: For I am on the road on which the Lord has guided me.

[Genesis 28:16]

LILLIAN: I have seen a divine being face to face, yet my life has been preserved.

[Genesis 32:31]

JERILYN: *Sh'ma Yisra'el, Adonai Eloheynu, Adonai Echad.* Hear, O Israel, the Lord our God, the Lord is One.

Immersion

JERILYN: *Baruch Atah Adonai, Eloheynu Yotzer ha'olam, asher kid'shanu b'mitzvotav vitzivanu al hatvilah.* Blessed art Thou, Lord our God, Creator of the world, who has made us holy with your commandments, and commanded us concerning immersion.

FRAN: Rid yourselves of the alien gods in your midst, purify yourselves, and change your garments. Let us promptly go up to Bethel and I will build an altar there to the God who answered me when I was in distress and who has been with me wherever I have gone.

[Genesis 35:2, from the week's Torah portion]

[Jerilyn recites the immersion prayer a second time.]

Immersion

JERILYN: *Baruch Atah Adonai, Eloheynu Ru-ach ha'olam, she-hechiyanu, v'kimanu, v'higgianu lazman ha'zeh.*

ALL: Blessed art Thou, Lord our God, Spirit of the world, who has kept us alive and sustained us and enabled us to reach this day.

Immersion

RABBI: *T'var-khekh Shekhinah vehtish-merekh. Ta'er Shekhinah pane-hhah eh-lei-ikh veh-teh-hunekh. Tisa Shekhinah paneh-hah eh-lei-ikh veh-tah-sem lakh shalom.* May God bless you and protect you. May the light of God shine upon you and God's grace be with you. May God be always with you and bring you peace. AMEN. *[The Priestly Blessing, with 'Shekhinah' substituted for 'Adonai'; and 'you' grammatically changed in Hebrew so that the prayer is bestowed upon a female rather than, as is traditional, upon a male.]*

[Note two changes in the Hebrew prayers: The word "Creator" and later "Spirit" are substituted for the word "King."]

Mikvah Ceremony for Laura

LAURA LEVITT AND RABBI SUE ANN WASSERMAN

Introduction

LAURA: The ceremony that follows was put together for me by my friend and my rabbi Sue Ann Wasserman after my rape in November 1989. The ceremony marks my particular experience and desire to heal. It is a ritual that speaks to the specific place I had come to in my healing on November 24, 1989. I went to the *mikvah*[1] with Sue Ann and my mother a few days after my first period after the rape. It was the day after Thanksgiving during my parents' first visit. It was erev Shabbat. Since November I have had other ways of marking time since the rape. My body has overcome a multitude of diseases punctuated by visits to doctors. This has been ongoing. I just took my second HIV test.[2] I have had to wait over six months for definitive results. Although I have maintained my professional life from the beginning, both teaching and studying, it has taken much time to recover other aspects of my life. I have slowly resumed having a fantasy life and a sex life, but I still long for a time when I will be able to live alone again.

SUE ANN: Although I grew up in a religious Reform Jewish home, *mikvah* was not a part of my background. I became interested in *mikvah* and the laws of family purity[3] while in rabbinic school. My interest stemmed from my need and desire to find parts of my tradition that spoke to me as a woman. I read and wrote and thought about *mikvah* as a woman's ritual both past and present. My practical knowledge of *mikvah* has come through my work with people who are converting to Judaism. I became convinced of its power to provide a meeting place for people and God, through listening to my students speak about their experience and how significant the *mikvah* was as a conclusion to their formal study for conversion.[4]

LAURA: Healing is a process. This *mikvah* ceremony is distinct in that it represents one of the few ways that I have been able to attend to my spiritual as well as my physical and emotional healing. Sharing this ceremony with other Jewish women is part of this healing. It is a way for me to give something of myself to other Jewish women, especially those who have been sexually abused. I want them to know that they are not alone. I also want them to know that there is a place for us and even our most painful experiences to be commemorated in Jewish community/ies.

My body was violated by rape. The *mikvah* offered me a place to acknowledge both that violation and my desire to heal. My need for ritual was very real. I needed to do something concrete to express my psychic and physical pain as a Jewish woman among other Jewish women I am close to.

For me, healing is not simply a return to some "wholeness" in the past; it is an experience of growth and change. Healing is the careful rebuilding of a life in the present that does not deny what has happened.

SUE ANN: When Laura was raped, I wanted to find a way to support her as her friend. As a rabbi, I needed to find a way for Judaism to respond to her. The *mikvah* seemed to be the most appropriate ritual for several reasons. (1) It was predominantly our foremothers' ritual. (2) It requires the whole body. (3) Its waters flow in and out—representing continuity and process. (4) Its waters symbolically flow from Eden, a place of wholeness. (5) The natural waters remind us of the constant intermingling presence of the Creator in our own lives. (6) Finally, water itself is cleansing, supportive, and life-sustaining.

The task then was to find words that would give this ancient ritual meaning in the context of Laura's experience. I drew on the sources at hand and included my own words as well as asking Laura to bring whatever readings she thought would be healing for her.

LAURA: The poems I chose to read during the *mikvah* ceremony reflect these feelings. Like the narrator in Irena Klepfisz's "Di rayze aheym" (The journey home),[5] I too wanted to return "home" but knew that the home I knew before the rape was no longer accessible to me. Nevertheless, I still needed a home. Healing has meant that I have had to rebuild a new life where I can attend to my scars while also experiencing joy again. I have had to rebuild my life "even from a broken web."[6] These words, the poetry of contemporary Jewish women, have helped me articulate some of these feelings, but to speak them at the *mikvah* made them physically tangible.

Historically, the *mikvah* is a sacred space for Jewish women and our bodies. Through this ceremony, I was able to enter into that tradition. Sue Ann helped me reconstitute this place to attend to my own physical needs for healing. In a steamy room overlooking a pool of running water in a synagogue in Atlanta, we recited these words and I entered the water. In so doing, the violation of my Jewish female body was attended to. It was neither silenced nor ignored.

SUE ANN: We stood together at the *mikvah*, the three of us, reading a liturgy that had been created in a day, to prepare us to perform a ritual that has existed for centuries. It was a powerful and empowering experience, but it was only a first step in the creation of a new liturgy that will speak to those who seek healing after a rape or any form of sexual abuse.

"Mikvah Ceremony for Laura"

SUE ANN: According to the Talmud, the ultimate source of all water is the river that emerged from Eden. By immersing ourselves in the *mikvah*, we participate in the wholeness of Eden. Natural water is required for a *mikvah* because water is a symbol of the life forces of the universe. Fundamentally, *mikvah* is not about "uncleanliness" but about human encounters with the power of the holy.[7]

To be read around by paragraph:
"In our tradition, water has always played a pivotal role. There is something elemental about it. Before the world was created, there existed the presence of God hovering over the surface of the water.

"When, in the times of Noah, God wished to make a new beginning of life on earth, the fountains of the deep were opened and waters came forth, returning the earth to its pristine beginnings.

"Our patriarchs and matriarchs met at the well, for the source of water was the center of community life. Thus the well, the source of water, marked the promise of new beginnings in their lives.

"Water is also a sign of redemption in our People's history. It was the waters of the Red Sea that parted and allowed us to go forth from bondage into freedom.

"Water is also a symbol of sustenance. Miriam, the sister of Moses, was deemed to be so righteous, that during her lifetime, when the Israelites wandered in the wilderness, God caused a well, Miriam's well it was called, to accompany the people and sustain them with water."[8]

LAURA: "Anger and tenderness: my selves.
And now I can believe they breathe in me
as angels, not polarities.
Anger and tenderness: the spider's genius
to spin and weave in the same action
from her own body, anywhere—
even from a broken web."[9]

(Laura reads)
"Di rayze aheym" (The journey home), by Irena Klepfisz[10]

SUE ANN: This ceremony is to help bring closure to your physical healing and cleansing. Your physical injuries are fading. You've done much cleaning; your apartment, your body, with soaps and masks, and miraculously your body has cleansed itself through menstruation.

This ceremony is also an attempt to help you begin the spiritual and emotional healing you must do. I see these *mikvah* waters as symbolic of two things. First, the tears you have yet to cry. Perhaps being surrounded by them from the outside will release them from the inside. Second, we do not sink in water but rather are buoyed up by it. It supports us gently. This is like your community of friends and family who have kept you afloat and sustained you. We, like the waters, are messengers of the Shechinah.[11] The Divine Presence is made present in your life through our loving and embracing arms and through the warm caress of these living waters.

LAURA: Now, as I immerse myself, I begin a new cycle in my life. May my entry into the waters of the *mikvah* strengthen me for the journey that lies ahead.[12]

> "Water is God's gift to living souls,
> to cleanse us, to purify us,
> to sustain us and renew us."[13]

SUE ANN: "May the God whom we call *Mikveh Yisrael*, and God who is the source of living waters, be with you now and always."[14]

The Immersion

Immersion and then recite:

בָּרוּךְ אַתָּה, יְיָ אֱלֹהֵינוּ, מֶלֶךְ הָעוֹלָם, אֲשֶׁר קִדְּשָׁנוּ בְּמִצְוֹתָיו וְצִוָּנוּ עַל הַטְּבִילָה.

Baruch ata Adonai Eloheynu Melech Ha-olam asher kid'shanu, bemitzvotav vitsivanu al ha'tevilah.

Blessed are You, *Adonai*, Ruler of the Universe, who sanctifies us with your commandments and commanded us concerning immersion.

Immersion and then recite:

בָּרוּךְ אַתָּה, יְיָ אֱלֹהֵינוּ, מֶלֶךְ הָעוֹלָם, שֶׁהֶחֱיָנוּ וְקִיְּמָנוּ וְהִגִּיעָנוּ לַזְּמַן הַזֶּה.

Baruch ata Adonai, Eloheynu Melech Ha-olam she-hechiyanu vikiamanu vihigianu lazman hazeh.

Blessed are You, *Adonai,* Ruler of the Universe, who kept us alive and preserved us and enabled us to reach this season.

Immersion for a third and final time.

Following the Immersion

Read around by stanzas:

"God give us the strength
    to transcend setbacks and pain
    to put our difficulties into perspective

God give us the strength
    to fight against all forms of injustice,
    whether they be subtle or easily apparent

God give us the strength
    to take the path less traveled
    and more disturbing

God give us the strength
    to persevere
    to reach out to those in need—
        may we abandon none of your creations

May we never become callous or apathetic because
    of our own disappointments

May our personal pain never be used as
    an excuse to stop heeding your call

God give us the strength
    to continually strive to do more

Let us always strive to give, even if we,
ourselves, feel alone or impoverished

For we must always strive to reach beyond
ourselves."[15]

Notes

1. *Mikvah* has many meanings in Hebrew. It is a confluence of water, a reservoir, a pool, or a ritual bath. *Mikvah* is also understood to be a source of hope and trust, another name for God. The *mikvah* ceremony refers to the ritual of immersion in such a place for purposes of ritual purification. According to *halakhah,* Jewish law, the ritual of immersion is required for conversion to Judaism, but it is most commonly associated with "laws of family purity." Within monogamous heterosexual Jewish marriages, "as menstruation begins, a married couple halts all erotic activities. A minimum of five days are considered menstrual, then seven 'clean' days are observed with the same restrictions. After nightfall of the seventh day, the woman bathes herself . . . and immerses herself in a special pool built to exacting specifications" (Susan Weidman Schneider, *Jewish and Female: A Guide and Sourcebook for Today's Jewish Woman* [New York: Touchstone, 1985], 204; see pp. 203–13 for an extended discussion of the ritual and its revival).

2. HIV, the human immunodeficiency virus, is believed to be the cause of AIDS, acquired immunodeficiency syndrome. HIV is a blood-borne virus transmitted through the exchange of bodily fluids.

3. See n. 1 above.

4. *Mikvah* is a part of the traditional conversion process. To convert to Judaism one must engage in formal study of the tradition and, having done so for a significant period of time, must agree to take on the obligations of the tradition. According to *halakhah,* the ceremony that marks this transition is *mikvah.* Immersion concretizes the transformation that has already been achieved through study and obligation. In Reform Judaism, ritual immersion is an optional part of the conversion process.

5. Melanie Kaye/Kantrowitz and Irena Klepfisz, eds., *The Tribe of Dina: A Jewish Women's Anthology* (Montpelier, Vt.: Sinister Wisdom 29/30, 1986), 49–52.

6. Adrienne Rich, *A Wild Patience Has Taken Me This Far: Poems, 1978–1981* (New York: Norton, 1981), 9.

7. Anita Diamant, *The New Jewish Wedding* (New York: Summit, 1985), 151.

8. Jeffrey Perry-Marx, "A Ceremony of Tevilih," unpublished manuscript used in a senior rabbinic workshop on outreach given by Rabbi Nina Mizrachi at Hebrew Union College–Jewish Institute for Religion, New York, spring 1987.

9. Rich, 9.

10. Kaye/Kantrowitz and Klepfisz, 49–52.

11. The Shechinah is the Divine Presence in the world, the in-dwelling or immanent presence of God. Jewish mystical literature describes this presence as female. In the mystical tradition, the Shechinah is the feminine principle of God to be found in the world.

12. From "A Bridal Mikvah Ceremony," by Barbara Rossman Penzener and Amy Zwiback-Levenson, in Diamant, *The New Jewish Wedding,* 157–58.

13. Ibid.

14. Perry-Marx, "A Ceremony of Tevilih."

15. This prayer was written by Angela Graboys and Laura Rappaport. It is found in a daily service they edited, "ROW Service," an unpublished manuscript, Cincinnati, Hebrew Union College–Jewish Institute of Religion. ROW is an organization for women rabbinical students at Hebrew Union College–Jewish Institute of Religion in Cincinnati.

A Ritual of Loss
For Rosh Hodesh, Tammuz (*June/July*):
A Time to Mourn

PENINA ADELMAN

BRING: Copies of the story of Hannah; an object of good fortune or protection (a hamsa or mizrach) [good luck charm, used as protection for the home] which could be jointly made/given by members of the group to support and strengthen the woman who is the subject of the ritual. (As preparation, read the myth of Tammuz;[1] and the story of Hannah in 1 Sam. 1:1–2.)

SETTING: At the home of the woman for whom the ritual of healing is intended. Since this ritual will touch upon the very painful issues of loss and grieving, care must be taken to assure that its location is a safe place, free from distractions or noise. Selecting an outdoor area is not encouraged.

Themes of Tammuz

Keeper: The name of this month, *Tammuz,* recalls an ancient myth of death and rebirth—when a descent into the depths is made as a means of fructification. To find traces of the rituals of *Tammuz,* we look in the Book of Ezekiel:

> Then he brought me to the door of the gate of the Lord's house which was towards the north; and behold, there sat women weeping for Tammuz. [Ezek. 8:14]

According to Sumerian tradition, Tammuz was a beautiful young god or god-like man who died and was then brought back to life with the aid of his sister, Innini. The myth of the dying and rising god, Tammuz, became transformed in Judaism into the destruction and rebuilding of the Holy Temple, the cyclical annihilation and rejuvenation of the Jewish people. This rhythm pervades the history of the Jews.

Several historical events occur in *Tammuz,* marking this month as a time of despair and mourning for the Jewish people. On the 17th of *Tammuz,* Noah sent a dove from the ark to scout for land, but the bird found no place to rest (Gen. 8:9). On the same day, when Moses returned from the top of the mountain, he broke the Tablets of the Law after finding his people worshipping the golden calf (Exod. 32:19). During the time of the First and Second Temples, the walls of Jerusalem were breached by the enemy. The 17th of *Tammuz* signifies the beginning of a three-week period of intense mourning which culminates in the Ninth of *Av, Tisha B'Av,* the date when both the First and the Second Temples were destroyed. That day has since become a minor fast day.

Sign of *Tammuz*

Keeper: The sign of this month is *Sartan,* the Crab. The crab echoes the major theme of *Tammuz* for it scrapes away at the earth in its search for food, remains buried for a time, and later returns above ground to continue its journey.

Kavannah

Grieving for pregnancy-loss or infertility.

The reader should be aware of the potentially broad applications of the following ritual. In the one presented, the loss is that of a fetus through miscarriage. Our ritual might serve as a stimulus to anyone who has suffered the loss of a child, a parent, a spouse, a relationship, a pregnancy. Society regularly marks the death of a human being, but not necessarily the end of a period of grief. The end of a marriage in divorce, the death of an unborn child, the abortion of a fetus, and the loss of a lover—all require a period of mourning. These events are seldom ritualized. We believe time must be set aside for this.

The following *Avedah* ritual is one example of a woman dealing with a loss which society does not recognize or validate.

Keeper: Tonight, with your help, I would like to perform a ritual to acknowledge an important event in my life. One year ago this month, I lost a pregnancy. My personal loss is reflected in the very character of the month of *Tammuz* during which the life force is snuffed out in the person of the god of vegetation, Tammuz. It is also the month in which began the destruction of Jerusalem, the spiritual center of the Jewish people. I, too, lost my spiritual center when I lost my potential child. My very womanhood seemed to be in jeopardy since I could not continue to carry a child.

There are no rituals within Judaism to mark the loss of a pregnancy. For my own spiritual survival, I had to dip into Miriam's Well to create one—based on the story of Hannah in the Bible, in the First Book of Samuel.

Every day since I lost my baby, I have turned to the Book of Samuel to study the story of Hannah, who suffered because she was unable to bear a child. I found solace, inspiration and meaning in her story.

The story of Hannah forms the basis for the *midrash* I wish to share with you as part of my *Avedah* ritual. This *midrash* is about creativity, individual and communal. It illustrates the idea that an individual is often unable to express innermost emotions or thoughts unless other sympathetic people witness them.

I was able to grieve and soul-search on my own, and then felt I needed to come to you with what I discovered, to make a statement as a group about this loss. My hope is that this ritual will heal wounds all of us bear as the result of losses we've experienced.

(A woman starts the ritual by singing a *niggun* and the rest join in. The music sets a mood of sadness, longing, quiet pain and underlying strength. The songs that follow contribute to this mood: *A mol iz geven a mayseh* [Yiddish folksong]; *Gesher Tsar Me' od.*)

Keeper: Let's read the story of Hannah together.

(Copies of 1 Sam. 1–2 are given. One woman reads the story aloud as the others silently follow. Then a discussion ensues, using these questions. Each group may frame their own or proceed.)

—What is the deeper meaning of the repeated biblical motif of two wives—one is fertile and one is barren, one is beautiful and one is ugly, one is righteous and one is unsavory? Examples are pairs such as Eve and Lilith, Sarah and Hagar, Rachel and Leah, Hannah and Peninnah, Esther and Vashti.

—Why is Hannah's prayer considered by the Rabbis to be the ideal form of prayer? Is this justified? What are your notions of prayer, ideal or mundane?

(After the women have discussed the story, the Keeper explains how she created a *midrash* from her own understanding of the text.)

Keeper: The stories in the Bible tell of many women who were infertile—they could not conceive a child. Infertility need not necessarily denote a physical state but rather a spiritual, emotional or mental state of barrenness. This is the teaching of Hannah, with its hint as to how one may change the barrenness to creation.

What I did with this story can be applied to any story in the Hebrew Bible. First, the reading of Hannah's story became for me a daily ritual of comfort and exploration. Each morning for a year I sat with this story and digested it, studied it, and was inspired by it. Each day I read another verse and pondered it, asking questions, struggling with it. Then I read commentaries on the story, mostly in *Pesikta Rabbati*, to see what the Rabbis thought about Hannah and her rival, Peninnah.[2] Finally I wrote my own version of the story. It was a synthesis of the original text, its commentaries, and my own answers to questions about it. Hannah began to speak to me through her ancient story, through rabbinic teachings, and through my own experience.

This ritual of studying Hannah's story became a *kaddish* which I said each day for my dead baby. In this way I was able to live through the loss instead of being consumed by it. The process I have described may be applied to any story which speaks to you in your own situation.

Torah Study

Keeper: When I looked carefully at Hannah's story, I noted that the turning point was her prayer. She can no longer tolerate her infertile state and is driven to "pour out her heart" before God. The text says,

Now Hannah was praying in her heart; only her lips moved, but her voice could not be heard. So Eli thought she was drunk (1 Sam. 1:13).

Of course, the priest who represented the religious establishment could not understand such heartfelt prayer and misinterpreted her behavior as inebriation and decadence.

Here, in Hannah's prayerful silence, the text demands of the reader an active imagination. What is Hannah saying to God? The silent narrative is an invitation for the reader to open up emotionally, as Hannah did, in order for inner healing to occur.

This is the basis for the *Avedah* ritual. I'll sing the ballad of Hannah and when I reach the part about her prayer, I shall stop and invite all to imagine what Hannah might have expressed.

What would you give to Hannah to help her focus her *kavannah* for this prayer to God, to help her shape her words after her long silence?

This ballad has a chorus with just two words, *Rachem Aleinu,* "have compassion for us." In Hebrew the word for compassion, *rachmanut,* and for womb, *rechem,* come from the same root. I've always thought that the wombs of women form a secret, silent network of communication all over the world. Every woman knows what it means to menstruate, to bear a child, to experience menopause. Every time a woman tells a story "from her womb," other women hearing the story feel it in their depths as well.

Ballad of Hannah[3]
(Tune: "Scarborough Fair"; Traditional English Folksong)

1. Once there lived a man named Elkanah,
"God has gotten" was his name,
He got two wives, this Elkanah,
Bitter rivals all the same.

The first one's name was Peninnah,
Precious pearl, Pe-nin-nah,
Mother of pearls, Pe-nin-nah,
Pearls in her womb, Pe-nin-nah.

The second one's name was Hannah,
Full of grace, Hannah

Full of love, Hannah
Full of longing, Hannah

Chorus: *Rachem aleinu* (in cantorial style)
   Rachem aleinu
   Rachem aleinu

For Peninnah had children while Hannah had none,
Peninnah had pearls while Hannah had none,
Peninnah had hope while Hannah had none,
Peninnah gave life while Hannah gave none.

Every morning, every day Peninnah would taunt her rival and say,
Have you fed your children breakfast?
Have you dressed them for school?
Have you taught them well the Golden Rule?

2. Hannah spoke not a word in return,
But deep inside, her heart did burn,
She thought, there must be more than this to life.
Than being a mother and a wife.

Chorus . . . *Rachem aleinu,* etc.

Years rolled by like unstrung pearls,
Peninnah kept having more boys and girls,
Hannah kept waiting for one seed to grow,
But her belly was filled with darkness and woe.

Hannah could not eat and she could not sleep,
All she could do was sit and weep
And mourn for the children who might have been.
She felt like a sinner without a sin.

Chorus . . . *Rachem aleinu,* etc.

Elkanah tried to understand
Why Hannah felt like a barren land.
"Am I not better than ten sons to you?
Let's count our blessings though they seem few."

That very year when they went up to pray
To the Lord of Hosts to bless their way,
Hannah did remain behind,
She had words in her heart, she had things on her mind.

Chorus . . . *Rachem aleinu,* etc.

(The Keeper stops singing at this point and invites the other women to give voice to Hannah's prayer in whatever way feels natural.)

Woman: Hannah, I'd like to give you some words from another woman who knew how to speak from her heart, Emily Dickinson. (She reads "Hope is the thing with feathers.")[4]

Woman: I have a "tune without words" for you, Hannah.[5] My mother used to sing it when she lit the candles on Friday night. I never heard her sing it—she died when I was two. My grandmother, who was not observant, who brought me up, sang it for me as she lit the Sabbath candles. And each time she would say, "I'm only lighting these candles and singing the tune for your mother, because she would have wanted you to know these things."[6]

This is important for you, Hannah, because the Rabbis read into the letters of your name—*chet, nun, heh*—an acronym for the three basic *mitzvot,* commandments, which are incumbent upon women. They are *hallah,* which starts with the letter *chet,* signifying the portion of bread which is to be set aside for the priest each week; *niddah,* which begins with the letter *nun,* meaning the laws of ritual purity a woman is to observe; and finally, *hadlakat nerot,* which begins with a *heh,* lighting candles on the Sabbath, which is the duty of the woman of the household. (She sings the remembered tune.)

Woman: I brought you this purple cord from Rachel's Tomb, Hannah. Brides and new mothers derive strength from the matriarch, Rachel. She also intercedes on behalf of women who have great difficulty bearing children.[7]

By coming together at this time to honor Hannah and Rachel, to think about their infertility and to remember their strength, adding it to our own, we become the "thirteenth stone" for the Tomb of Rachel.[8] This thirteenth stone, forgotten until now, represents the sisters of the Twelve Tribes, the daughters of Rachel and Leah who are here in spirit with us. As the *Midrash* states, "To each of the twelve tribes was born a sister, and to Benjamin were born two sisters."

Now is the time to reclaim the lost stone, the lost words of Hannah, the lost stories of Rachel and Leah and all our foremothers, the lost Torah of the Thirteen Sisters! Let their words resound throughout the land!

(The women take turns in reaffirming the meaning of the story.)

Woman: Hannah, wisdom grows in your womb like a child. We tell your story on the New Moon of *Tishre,* the greatest *Rosh Hodesh* of the year.[9]

Woman: The Rabbis saw in the letters of the words *Roshei Hodshim* the word *rechem,* womb. The circle of the year is a womb in which the seasons, the earth, the festivals, the sacred stories are born anew, again and again.

Woman: Life can be seen as a series of impregnations, labors, births, growths and then new conceptions, maturations over time. Each "impregnation" may be another coming to consciousness.

Woman: "Pregnancy" may be the stage of carrying an "issue" within, experiencing grief and growth. This is a time of change, confusion, fear, movement.

Woman: "Labor" is the period of struggling with resolution. That may be a painful time or a carefree one. If the birth is healthy, growth continues happily. If the stage of resolution or "birth" is not reached, one may have to begin again.

Woman: Hannah, this way of thinking has helped me. If I can't give birth to a live human being, I can give birth to the ideas and struggles within me.

Woman: Hannah, remember our foremothers, Sarah, Hagar, Rebecca, Rachel and Leah; how they, too, wrestled with barrenness and fertility. Let them teach us how to gain strength through our common struggle.

(After the women have offered words to Hannah, the Keeper concludes the story by way of prose narrative and ballad.)

Keeper of *Tammuz:* Eli, the priest, was incensed by the myriad voices he heard in the sanctuary. He told Hannah to be gone, to take her drunkenness elsewhere.

But Hannah explained to him that she had not been drinking, saying, "I have been pouring out my soul before God."

Then Eli was struck by her sorrowful, heartfelt words. He had not been able to pray for years and her words opened his heart so that he felt like praying. Her words were pearls, stringing themselves from her heart to his ears. He told her to go back to her husband and tell him what she had just said. Soon, promised Eli, she would have a child.

Hannah returned to Elkanah and told him all she had told the priest. Her husband was overcome by sadness. "Hannah, I never understood your agony at not having children. Tell your story to Peninnah." This was done, and Peninnah, too, was touched by her rival's pains. She embraced Hannah. Soon after Hannah bore a son. Word of Hannah's marvelous gift spread quickly. When people came to tell her their problems, she responded with words which were pearls reaching from her heart to their ears.

Ballad
So Hannah bore many words,
She only spoke what she heard.
Inside her grew numerous pearls
Those words became her boys and girls.

The first one's name was Shmuel,
"His name is God"—Shmuel,
Every word a name of God—Shmuel.
Every word a pearl—Shmuel.

Now my story has come to an end
As Peninnah and Hannah on each other depend,
For pearls are formed in the womb of grace
Where the fertile and the barren learn to embrace.

Chorus . . . *Rachem aleinu,* etc.

The women are visibly moved by Hannah's tale. One woman introduces the concept of group wailing.

Group Wailing

Woman: I feel that the tears of Hannah are palpable in the air here and so I would like to try weeping together as did the professional mourning women of old.

(She sings a mournful *niggun,* a wordless tune. It is not necessary to have a specific tune in mind. One can begin the group wailing simply by moaning over and over again. This often opens one up to weeping as does the sound of others' moans. This activity will not suit everyone. Those who are uncomfortable with it should be encouraged to remain silent or sit outside the circle. For those who are willing, group wailing is a way to express bottled-up grief in a safe environment. Each group intuitively finds its own rhythm of wailing, rising to a crescendo, a high intensity, and then fading to a *niggun* and to relaxed breathing. A *niggun* in the "blues" mode is very appropriate to this activity. The group wailing ends and there is silence for several moments.)

Singing

The Keeper now sits in the center of the room. The women stand, circling around her, singing songs of fruitfulness and compassion, restoration and rebuilding. As they sing, the woman who is marking her loss may become the center of a final ritual of healing. The women place their hands on her womb, heart and head.

Suggestions for songs: *HaNitsamim; Yibaneh Ha Mikdash; Rakhmana D'Anyee* (Liturgy—Hasidic melody); *Yerushalayim, M'Harbanotayikh Evneh;* The Water Lily.[10]

When they have finished singing, refreshments are served. The Keeper has completed the Ritual of Hannah, the climax of a year of mourning.

Notes

1. Variants of this myth are found among peoples of the ancient Near East as well as the Greeks and Romans. Tammuz is also known as Attis, Adonis, Dammuzi, Osiris, and Persephone. Innini is known as Cybele, Vanus, Ishtar, Isis, and Demeter. The myth has several possible origins. One may stem from the practice of child sacrifice during a time of distress or disaster, when a ruler might offer up his child to the gods as a means of appeasement. Or the myth of Tammuz may originate from the cycle of nature, as crops die during midsummer and resume in the rainy season, so does Tammuz descend to the underworld, reemerging later as a living being. The myth of Tammuz may be found in Stephen Herbert Langdon's "Tammuz," included in the collection *The Mythology of All Races* (Boston: Marshall Jones, 1931), 7:336–51. See also Diane Walkstein and Samuel Kramer, *Inanna* (New York: Harper & Row, 1983).

2. *Pesikta Rabbati*, Piska 43, pp. 752–68.

3. *Midrash*/Ballad of Hannah by P. V. Adelman, 1983.

4. From *The Complete Poems of Emily Dickinson,* ed. Thomas H. Johnson (Boston: Little, Brown, 1960), 254.

5. Ibid.

6. Story collected from Maia Brumberg at a *Rosh Hodesh* celebration in Boston, 1981.

7. For a different use of the cord from Rachel's Tomb, see the *Adar Aleph*.

8. For more on the custom of adding a stone to a gravesite during a visit to honor the dead, see *Encyclopaedia Judaica* (Jerusalem: Keter, 1972), S.V. "Holy Places," 8:922.

9. The story of Hannah is read each year as the *haftarah* for the first day of *Rosh Hashanah*.

10. Folk song on the album *The Water Lily* by Priscilla Herdman.

Healing Ritual for Abused Women

FAITH ROGOW

When a battered woman first seeks counseling or enters a shelter, she could join a counselor in saying the blessing for delivery from danger:

> Blessed are You, Holy One, Source of life, who bestows great goodness on me.
> Amen.

Or she could affirm the beginning of her new life by reciting *Shehecheyanu*:

> Blessed are You, Holy One, Source of life, who has kept us alive, sustained us, and brought us to this day. Amen.

The second step would be to add a special prayer to a personal ritual the woman already performs, such as lighting Shabbat candles. Possible texts for such prayers appear below:

Holy One, bring me comfort,
For I have seen terror;
Cradle me and I will feel safe,
Heal me and I will become strong,
Nurture me and I will grow.
You have taught me that to do righteousness and justice
Is more acceptable to You than sacrifice.
You have taught me that, with You beside me,
Fear is not eternal.

Help me to live by Your teachings.
Blessed are You, Holy One, Source of life,
Who guides us, who protects us, who sustains us.
Amen.

Based on Psalms 6 and 21

In distress I called on the Source of life,
You answered me and brought me relief.
God is on my side,
I have no fear;
What can man do to me?
With God on my side as my helper,
I will overcome my foes. . . .
I shall not die, but live
And proclaim the works of the Holy One!

Psalm 118:5–7, 17

As with the Mourner's *Kaddish,* this added prayer is meant to ease
the woman out of her distress and, like the *Kaddish,* could be read as
part of a yearlong cycle—weekly for six months and then monthly for
six months. The final recitation of the cycle might be marked as a
quiet victory celebration. The following, a reinterpretation of a text
traditionally understood to applaud subservient rather than independent women, might be added to or replace the text the woman had been
reading:

I am a woman of valor,
My arms are new with strength.
My hands will plant vineyards;
With dignity will I tend them,
With laughter and with wisdom will I make them grow;
And I will seek goodness all the days of my life.

Based on Proverbs 31

It would be appropriate for the woman to read this aloud to a small
circle of friends, perhaps at a Shabbat dinner they have made for her. The
group could respond with the phrase *Chazak Chazak v'nitchazeik,*

"From strength to strength are we strengthened." Here, as in the phrase's traditional context (the completion of public reading of a book of the Torah), the words remind us that new insight brings new power.

The woman should also be encouraged to make a contribution in time, goods, or money to her local crisis center or shelter for battered women as an expression of her new strength and as an acknowledgment that she participates in the ongoing cycle of healing, as a healer as well as one healed.

Laying *T'fillin*: A Ritual
of Emotional Healing for Men

RABBI ALLAN C. TUFFS

Men are often accused of being out of touch with their emotions. Ask a man what he is feeling at a given moment and he is likely to look at you blankly. Even when suffering emotional distress, many men will say that they are "just fine." The language of the heart is a foreign idiom to most men. Men are more fluent in the language of thinking, problem solving, and conceptualizing.

Perhaps thinking comes more easily than emoting to men as a result of their hard wiring. In the hunter food-gathering days of human history, too much emotion may have diminished a man's ability to track and kill his prey. Subsequent human cultures, with their need for soldiers and strong-backed workers, undoubtedly reinforced masculine stoicism.

In modern times, we have learned that men pay a terrible price when they suppress their emotions. Heart disease, drug addiction, suicide, and a life expectancy eight years shorter than women are part of the symptomatology of men's estrangement from their feelings.

Our religious tradition suggests a more holistic vision for men that integrates the mind, body, and heart in the service of God. The following is a meditation for men on the wearing of the *tallit* and *t'fillin*. The goal of this four-part meditation is to help men be more in touch with their feelings by integrating the physical, emotional, and intellectual aspects of their psyches. (Note: you may want to record these meditations and play them back while doing them.)

Meditation on the *Tallit*

It is preferable to do this meditation outdoors, in as natural a setting as possible. If you are lucky enough to live near a forest, a beach, or a desert, you may choose to do this meditation there. If you live in a city or a suburb, as most of us do, you might use your backyard, patio, or a balcony. Be somewhere you can see the sky and feel the air on your skin.

Blessing

As you envelop yourself in the *tallit,* say the following blessing:

בָּרוּךְ אַתָּה, יְיָ אֱלֹהֵינוּ, מֶלֶךְ הָעוֹלָם, אֲשֶׁר קִדְּשָׁנוּ
בְּמִצְוֹתָיו וְצִוָּנוּ לְהִתְעַטֵּף בַּצִּיצִית.

Baruch atah Adonai, Eloheinu Melech haolam, asher kid'shanu b'mitzvotav v'tzivanu l'hitateif batzitzit.

Blessed are You, *Adonai,* Sovereign of the universe, who has sanctified us with mitzvot and has commanded us to envelop ourselves in the *tallit.*

Meditation

Close your eyes and focus on your breathing. Notice how the breath enters and exits your body without any intention or effort on your part. The word for "breath" and "soul" in Hebrew is the same word, *nefesh.* Your breathing is a spiritual dance between you and *Adonai.* You breathe in *Adonai,* the Source of your soul/breath, and *Adonai* breathes you. Gently bring your mind to focus all its attention on the simple act of breathing. *(2–3 minutes)*

Now bring your attention to your body. Notice the air around you, its temperature and where it touches your exposed skin. Take note of what is happening in your body at this time. What parts of your body are comfortable? Which parts of your body are uncomfortable? You need not do anything right now. Just be aware of your body. *(2–3 minutes)*

Notice the sounds in your environment. Listen without identifying anything. If your mind begins to create visual images or stories about those sounds, gently bring it back to the act of listening intently. *(2–3 minutes)*

Now become aware of the smells around you. Do not identify them or evaluate them; just experience them. If your mind begins to take you to another place or time in the past or in the future, gently bring it back and be totally aware of the fragrances around you in this place and at this time. *(2–3 minutes)*

Now open your eyes, and without fixing your gaze on any particular object, become aware of colors, shapes, and shades. Do not put words to anything you see, and do not identify anything. Simply experience what you see. If your mind begins to wander, gently bring it back to the act of seeing. Allow your peripheral vision to grow in all directions—up, down, right, and left. *(2–3 minutes)*

Prayer

Adonai, I stand before You, my body held and embraced by this *tallit.* I feel Your healing Presence in every fiber of my being. May I always use my physical powers to sanctify Your name.

Meditation on the *T'fillin Shel Yad*

Place the *t'fillin shel yad* on your left arm.

Blessing

בָּרוּךְ אַתָּה, יְיָ אֱלֹהֵינוּ, מֶלֶךְ הָעוֹלָם, אֲשֶׁר קִדְּשָׁנוּ
בְּמִצְוֹתָיו וְצִוָּנוּ לְהָנִיחַ תְּפִלִּין.

Baruch atah Adonai, Eloheinu Melech haolam, asher kid'shanu b'mitzvotav v'tzivanu l'haniach t'fillin.

Blessed are You, *Adonai*, Sovereign of the universe, who sanctified us with mitzvot and has commanded us to wear *t'fillin*.

Meditation (5–7 minutes)

Become aware of the *t'fillin* on your left arm; it is beside your heart. As you allowed yourself to be aware of your physical senses during the meditation on the *tallit*, now give yourself permission to be aware of your emotions. Without defining, labeling, or judging, simply allow yourself to experience any emotion that you have at this moment. Notice the interplay between your emotions and your body. If you are experiencing anger, how does your body react? If you are feeling shame or guilt, where in your body are these expressed? If you are excited about something, where do you feel it? If you are in love, how does your body express it? How does sadness express itself in your body?

Be aware of the interplay between thinking and emotions. Think of something important going on in your life right now. Perhaps it concerns a relationship, your health, or some issue in your work life. Focus on that issue. Live with it in your mind for a moment. What emotional responses were evoked? What physical responses were evoked?

Now focus on your breathing again. Allow the visual image in your mind that evoked those emotional and physical responses to retreat to the sidelines, where they might be dispersed like small wispy clouds on a warm summer day. Once more you have returned to a peaceful, calm place within yourself.

Prayer

Adonai, I thank You for the power that my emotions give me. My emotions give nuance and color to my life. The ability to exalt in the joy of living and to grieve the losses that are inevitable in life bring me closer to You. May I always use my emotions to sanctify Your name.

Meditation on the T'fillin Shel Rosh

Place the t'fillin shel rosh on your forehead.

Blessing

בָּרוּךְ אַתָּה, יְיָ אֱלֹהֵינוּ, מֶלֶךְ הָעוֹלָם, אֲשֶׁר קִדְּשָׁנוּ
בְּמִצְוֹתָיו וְצִוָּנוּ עַל־מִצְוַת תְּפִלִּין.

Baruch atah Adonai, Eloheinu Melech haolam, asher kid'shanu b'mitzvotav v'tzivanu al mitzvat t'fillin.

Blessed are You, *Adonai*, Sovereign of the universe, who has sanctified us with mitzvot and has commanded us concerning *t'fillin*.

Meditation (5–7 minutes)

The next few minutes are for meditating on what happens in your mind. You might ask, how can I be an objective observer of my own mind? If my mind is engaged in the act of thinking, with what do I observe my mind?

There is part of your mind that is always thinking. It imagines and analyzes. It creates visual images and inner dialogues within itself. However, there is another part of your mind that can be somewhat detached from all of this noise and activity. Think of that part of your mind as a "mind behind the mind." That part of your mind can help you decide whether or not you want to think about something. It helps you recognize the emotional and physical effects of a thought. If the effect is negative, you can decide not to think that thought.

Allow your eyes to close. You may focus on your breathing for a moment to center yourself. Become aware of the *t'fillin shel rosh* on your forehead. It is there to remind you that your thoughts are there for you to respond to in any way you choose. It reminds you that you are able to direct your thoughts in any direction you wish. Your thoughts belong to you. You do not belong to your thoughts.

Allow yourself to dwell for the next few moments in "the mind behind the mind," that place where you can observe your thoughts objectively, without being attached and carried away by them. Notice any thought you may be having at this time. Does this thought concern an event that has already taken place? Does it concern an event in the future you are anticipating? What is the nature of that thought? Is it visual or auditory? If it is visual, what are its shapes, colors, and contours? If it is auditory, is it reassuring or chastising? Notice the reaction of your body to that thought. Notice your emotional response to it.

As you observe that thought, become aware of your breathing. Repeat several times in a soft voice, "Breath arising, breath falling away." As you internalize the rhythm of your breathing with these words, become aware of the rhythm of your thoughts as you say in a soft voice, "Thought arising, thought falling away." Know that you can observe your thoughts without being attached to them. You can redirect your thoughts in new directions or even choose not to think about them at all at this time.

Prayer

> *Adonai,* I thank You for the intellectual powers with which You have endowed me. Help me to use my mind in fulfilling Your will. May I use my thoughts to sanctify Your name.

Meditation on the Sh'ma (*3–5 minutes*)

For the next few moments, become aware of the *tallit* enveloping your body. Be aware of all sensations in your body. Bring your attention to the *t'fillin shel yad* on your left arm, beside your heart. Be aware of the emotions you are experiencing right now. Notice the interplay between your body and emotions. Now bring your attention to your mind. What thoughts are arising there? Notice the interplay between your mind, emotions, and body.

Now allow your consciousness to encompass all three aspects of your being—physical, emotional, and intellectual—at the same time. Hold that consciousness as long as you can, directing it toward God. This is what is meant by the word *echad* (one) in the *Sh'ma;* as God is One, so we seek to unite all aspects of our being in oneness in service of the Eternal.

Now repeat the *Sh'ma* seven times:

Sh'ma Yisrael Adonai Eloheinu, Adonai Echad.

Sit quietly for a few minutes and allow these words to penetrate every part of your being.

Mikveh and Embodiment:
Healing the Spirit after a Medical Scare

RABBI ELLIOT M. STROM

It was the image that sustained me through what I now think of as my "little medical scare." It was the image through all the uncertainty, anxiety, and fear, a vivid—almost physical—image of me floating in the waters of the *mikveh*, the salt water of my tears dissolving into the living waters of the *mikveh*, feeling release, feeling gratitude, feeling oneness with the waters around me. When the anxiety got especially bad, this image was the only thing that could calm me, the only thing that kept me going.

When I did indeed get the medical report I had prayed for, I went immediately to the *mikveh* with the hope of re-creating that powerful image in my head. I expected to find there a physical way to act out my relief and joy. I imagined it would be a truly spiritual experience. As is often the case in this unpredictable life we live, I got something other than what I expected, but something good and sustaining and even radiant in its own way.

It began when I slowly took off my dark suit, tie, and white shirt. Stripped naked, I turned to examine my body in the mirror—as if it were the body of another. It looked remarkably healthy; after my previous anxiety, that was reassuring indeed.

I then entered the shower, turned it up as hot as it would go, and allowed it to play upon the tight muscles in my neck. Then I began, slowly and methodically, to wash myself. Acutely conscious of myself as a physical being, I decided I would soap every inch of my body. So I began to lather up everywhere, even struggling to get to those hard-to-reach places on my lower back. Then I rinsed off in the hot spray of the showerhead.

I liked the experience so much, I decided to do it once again—this time not for cleansing but for the sheer joy of it. Once again, I soaped up my body in its entirety. Once again, I luxuriated in the hot shower spray.

Now it was time to enter the *mikveh.* I closed the door behind me and descended the seven steps—deliberately counting each one in turn—and then stood in the waters of the *mikveh,* almost up to my neck. I had decided that I would "dip" three times, as I have instructed so many converts to do, reciting the *mikveh* blessing at the first immersion, the *Shehecheyanu* at the second, and the *Sh'ma* on the third.

Standing motionless for a moment, I knew what else I had to do. Before I descended under the water's surface, I ran my hands over my entire body, beginning with my scalp, my face, my chest and torso, then down my legs to my feet. I focused on the sensations as I got to know, really know, my body. Then and only then, when I was aware of my embodiment, conscious of the fact that God has placed my soul in a very vulnerable, yet surprisingly resilient body, only then did I let myself go under the water's surface.

Of course, I couldn't avoid the irony of the moment. While I had come to the *mikveh* expecting a powerful spiritual experience, what I was actually experiencing was the least spiritual and the most physical of sensations. It was sensual, powerfully sensual. For the first time in a long while, perhaps ever, I was truly aware of my "physicalness" and thankful for it. Having come to the *mikveh* out of fear that my physical body was under assault, I left feeling solid and strong and healthy—possessed not of a spiritual but a physical, body wisdom.

I felt good and thought maybe I should do this each month, just as some women choose to do. And even if my body—unlike theirs—doesn't function on a monthly cycle, I know that there are cycles in my life as well and there will undoubtedly be times in the future when I will want and need to be in the *mikveh*'s waters once again. But I know the *mikveh* is truly "living waters": it reflects, intensifies, and responds to the interior reality of the person in those waters.

I know I will come back again. I want to experience again the joy of "sheer embodiment" and to thank God for the gift of this vulnerable yet resilient home in which God causes my soul to dwell.

Ready for Redemption:
A *Mikveh* Experience of Personal Healing

RABBI STEVE Z. LEDER

"You can't put one *tuchus* in two chairs," was my father's not-so-quaint way of summing up times like the High Holy Days for rabbis. On one chair there's my own inner search for meaning among the ruins of last year's regrets and next year's promises. On the other, my responsibility to help lead thousands on their own inner journey—not to mention making the kids' school lunches each morning and cleaning up after the dog. Guess which chair wins?

One way or another though, I do find time to prepare for the High Holy Days. I check the prayer book to make sure I know all my parts and have my glasses adjusted so they don't slip down my nose when I preach. My robe and *tallis* are dutifully dry-cleaned, and my sermons are carefully rehearsed from the *bimah*.

But in the midst of all these technical preparations—and in the midst of getting the synagogue cranked up for another year of holiday celebrations, religious school, adult education, study groups, the men's group, the fund-raising, the late summer weddings, hospital visits, funerals, meetings, memos, and phone calls—there's not much time for personal reflection. In fact, even during the actual High Holy Day services I'm usually too preoccupied to do much serious praying and thinking.

The truth is these annual rituals of mine have more to do with being a rabbi who works during the High Holy Days than with being a Jew who prays. Any rabbi who tells you he or she can do both is at best an optimist and at worst racking up another white lie to add to next year's Yom Kippur confession.

I've confronted a lot of joy and sadness as a rabbi. Weddings, babies, miraculous recoveries, hugs from children, tears of joy—there's plenty of good to go around. But so too open wounds in the hospital, brain tumors in young fathers, divorce, murdered children—you name it. The problem is staying connected to it all. I can go from a wedding to a funeral to a *b'ris* in one day without thinking very much about it. It's not that I'm insensitive—just busy.

In part, I make my living helping Jews face sorrow. But it's their sorrow I help them through, and during the High Holy Days it's their self-scrutiny I try to facilitate, not my own. Yes, I've faced a lot of things as a rabbi, but it's not very often that I face myself. I'm no different from most people—rabbis, salesclerks, attorneys, bus drivers, doctors, tailors, teachers, and parents—we're all so busy living that it's hard to feel truly alive.

There was, however, that one afternoon the week before Rosh Hashanah thirteen years ago at the *mikveh*. The *mikveh* in my town is tended by a woman named Lillian, affectionately known among rabbis in town as the "*Mikveh* Lady."

I knew traditional women used the *mikveh* after menstruation, and others used it for conversions to Judaism, kashering dishes, and occasionally prior to Shabbat or the High Holy Days, but I had never actually been in one before. After witnessing the impact it had on the young woman I just converted, I was curious.

Looking at Lillian, I wondered, "Could I use the *mikveh?*"

"Of course," she said warmly as she let me in.

Lillian hangs around a lot of rabbis, and she's seen the power of the *mikveh* at work in many people's lives. She knew more about what was in store for me than I did.

"Take your time," she said with a knowing smile.

"Take your time," I thought to myself. Rabbis so seldom get to take their time at anything they do.

I showered, brushed my teeth, trimmed my nails—the Law requires that nothing come between me and the water that would surround me. Then, naked and alone, I entered the square, silent, blue-tiled chamber—built to talmudic specifications—to immerse myself three times and recite blessings.

I descended the seven steps, one for each day of Creation. Standing shoulder-high in the water, I gently lowered my head and pulled my knees to my chest. Floating in the warmth, I felt linked to generations of men and women who also sought refuge, sought God, sought themselves in the *mikveh*. Suspended in the liquid silence, I was suspended too in an eternal, infinite moment.

To my dismay I sighed a sigh of sorrow. A sigh for all the unfinished business of my life. A sigh for my grandfather whom I had not seen in thirty years—still alive, but cut off from me in some twisted family conflict I vaguely recall but do not understand.

A sigh for my brother, my little brother whom I could not protect from the harshness of the world. A sigh for my lost loves—where are they now? Where am I now? Another sigh for Israel—how far I am from her again this year. Will my wife's cancer ever come back? A sigh because I should be better, do more, study more, give more, write more, read more. What kind of a father am I? What kind of a man am I?

Distinct and separate demons awakened all at once; psychic baggage never unpacked, weight never shed nor even noticed, but heavy to bear. My sorrows pushed deep into the background were magically released to the untelling, all-knowing waters; to God.

The week before Rosh HaShanah 5748, I left that small, quiet place slowly, having uttered my High Holy Day prayers for the very first time in piety and truth. I left ready for redemption.

Now I go back each year, curling like an embryo beneath the still water, making peace with my longings, reminding myself of Lillian's advice: "Take your time, rabbi. Take your time."

VI

HOLIDAYS
AND HEALING

A Healing Resource for the
Jewish High Holiday Season: Psalm 27

RABBI SIMKHA Y. WEINTRAUB

From the first day of the Hebrew month of Elul, one month before Rosh HaShanah, to the last day of Sukkot, traditional Jews add Psalm 27 to their daily prayers. One would think that, since it is singled out for this season of repentance, the Psalm would focus on human short-comings and our resolve to do better in the coming year. But, the focus of Psalm 27 is confidence and security in the shelter of the Almighty (however one may understand these notions), an intimate relationship of care and protection, and a very concrete persistent request of God to rally against besieging foes.

Psalm 27 has much to offer those of us struggling with illness—whether as patient, family member or friend, or health care provider. Our difficult "balancing act" of acceptance and activism, of living in the moment but fighting for the future, finds expression in these ancient words attributed to King David. As you read it, see what phrases or ideas resonate for you; consider revisiting the Psalm, alone or with close ones, during this season of Return and Response. Perhaps it will trigger your own creative writing effort to articulate your deepest prayers. It may link you to a community and a tradition of support, faith, affirmation and hope.

A Psalm of David
Adonai is my Light and my Help;
whom shall I fear?
Adonai is the Strength of my life;
who can make me afraid?

When evil people draw near
to devour my flesh—
it is these foes and enemies
who stumble and fall.

Even if an army rises up against me,
my heart will have no fear!
Even if a whole war besets me,
I will still feel secure.

One thing I ask from Adonai,
one thing I seek:
to dwell in Adonai's house
all the days of my life,
to gaze upon the beauty of Adonai,
to explore Adonai's sanctuary.

Adonai will shelter me in a
Sukkah on an evil day;
Adonai will conceal me in the
secret shelter of a tent,
raise me up safely upon a rock.

My head is high above my
enemies around me;
I sacrifice in Adonai's tent,
to the blasts of trumpets,
singing and chanting a hymn to Adonai!

Adonai—*sh'ma*/hear my voice when I call!
Have mercy on me and respond!

You seek my heart,
my heart seeks You—
I seek Your Presence.

Do not hide Your face from me;
Do not turn Your servant away in anger!
You have always been my Help
so do not abandon me, do not forsake me,
my God, my Saving One.

Even if my father and mother
abandoned me,
Adonai would gather me in.

Teach me Your ways, Adonai,
Guide me on a straight and level path,
because of my watchful enemies.

Do not hand me over to my foes;
ignore the false witnesses and
unjust accusers
who rise up against me,
breathing violence.

I believe I will yet see Adonai's goodness
in the Land of Life.

Hope in Adonai!
Be strong inside, and let your heart be brave!
Yes, yes, hope in Adonai!

One Hundred Sixty-five
In the Sukkah

DEBBIE PERLMAN *z"l*

Sit beside me, Kind Visitor,
Between these billowing walls,
Broken light through roof branches:
Hold me fall breezes.

I invite You, Kind Healer,
To sit in my *sukkah,*
To rest in my presence
As I recline against Yours.

I invite You to sweeten these days
With the etrog's fragrance,
Tart and pleasing,
A boon to my weary senses.

I invite Your companions
Of hope and faith,
Healing and wishes,
Wholeness returned.

Allow my hospitality,
In this place of peace,
Where together we plan recovery,
Fragility turned to strength.

Blessing and Extending the Light:
A Ritual of Healing for the
Eight Nights of Hanukkah

RABBI SIMKHA Y. WEINTRAUB

Hanukkah comes at the darkest moments of the year—close to the winter solstice with its shortest day and longest night, at the point in the month when the moon is obscured. Our response is to light candles in an effort to draw light into the world and to appreciate even the humblest, tiniest flickers of light as a blessing. For those who are struggling with illness or other serious life challenges, sitting with this darkness and meditating upon the light can provide comfort, inspiration, and perspective.

Even if we ourselves and those near and dear to us are fortunate not to be suffering, Jewish tradition urges us to be mindful of all of those who are ill by praying with and for them. Our daily prayers include hope for physical cure and spiritual healing for our loved ones, as well as for those we do not know. Jewish healing is thus an ongoing communal enterprise, potent in its concern for anyone dealing with illness, rich in its influence on the pray-er, and valuable in its ability to encourage "horizontal," interpersonal support even if divine, "vertical" intervention seems alien or remote.

Our thoughts and prayers, of course, may be all the more effective when they are tied to the particular needs and hopes of those who are suffering. But how can this be practical, when the kinds of afflictions are numerous; the personalities, challenges, and resources of those who are ill so diverse; and the courses and prognoses of disease so shifting and unpredictable?

One way is to seek to step into the experience of people who are ill, to empathically explore the physical, emotional, psychological, and spiritual passages they travel. While no two people have precisely the same experiences, we offer eight commonly-shared junctures in the journey of illness. For each, we have selected verses from the Book of Psalms centered around images of light—for reflection, study, prayer, chanting, and/or meditation.

We suggest that each night of Hanukkah, just before lighting the candles, we all pray for those who are ill, focusing on a particular juncture in the journey. Trying to imagine what the experience might be like, recite or chant the verse from Psalms (or, if you are able/inclined, utilize the entire Psalm). And then offer your own prayer for those living with illness and in need of spiritual strength.

The greatest "Hanukkah gift" is light. May our prayers, *tz'dakah,* and deeds of loving-kindness spark hope and strength, and illumine lives with renewed meaning and direction.

אָז יִבָּקַע כַּשַּׁחַר אוֹרֶךָ וַאֲרֻכָתְךָ מְהֵרָה תִצְמָח.

Then shall Your light burst through like dawn, and Your healing spring up quickly.

Isaiah 58:8

Before lighting the candles, begin each night with the following:

Adonai/my God, Source of healing and hope, we dedicate this night of Hanukkah to those who (complete with appropriate line below). Give them and those who care for them rich blessings of strength and support, solace and determination. Illumine their lives with insight and guidance, and shine peace and serenity on their path.

Recite or chant the appropriate verse from Psalms, and then continue with the traditional ritual of lighting the candles.

The first night of Hanukkah: . . . **are experiencing pain or symptoms**

יְהֹוָה אוֹרִי וְיִשְׁעִי מִמִּי אִירָא

יְהֹוָה מָעוֹז חַיַּי מִמִּי אֶפְחָד.

Adonai is my Light and my Salvation—whom will I fear?
Adonai is the Strength of my life—who can make me afraid?

(Psalm 27:1)

The second night of Hanukkah: . . . **are moving through tests
and evaluations**

כִּי־אַתָּה תָּאִיר נֵרִי

יְהֹוָה אֱלֹהַי יַגִּיהַּ חָשְׁכִּי.

It is You who lights my candle,
Adonai, my God, illumines the darkness.

(Psalm 18:29)

The third night of Hanukkah: . . . **are receiving a diagnosis**

גּוֹל עַל־יְהֹוָה דַּרְכֶּךָ וּבְטַח

עָלָיו וְהוּא יַעֲשֶׂה.

וְהוֹצִיא כָאוֹר צִדְקֶךָ

וּמִשְׁפָּטֶךָ כַּצָּהֳרָיִם.

Leave your way to Adonai,
Trust in Adonai, who will do it.
Adonai will cause your vindication to shine forth like the
    light,
the justice of your case like noonday sun.

(Psalm 37:5–6)

The fourth night of Hanukkah: . . . **are receiving treatments**

שְׁלַח־אוֹרְךָ וַאֲמִתְּךָ
הֵמָּה יַנְחוּנִי
יְבִיאוּנִי אֶל־הַר־קָדְשְׁךָ
וְאֶל־מִשְׁכְּנוֹתֶיךָ.

Send forth Your light and Your truth—
They will lead me;
They will bring me to Your holy mountain.
Your dwelling-place.

(Psalm 43:3)

The fifth night of Hanukkah: . . . **are undergoing surgery**

כִּי־עִמְּךָ מְקוֹר חַיִּים
בְּאוֹרְךָ נִרְאֶה־אוֹר.

With You is the source of life;
in Your light do we see light.

(Psalm 36:10)

The sixth night of Hanukkah: . . . **are recovering from surgery
and/or treatments**

כִּי הִצַּלְתָּ נַפְשִׁי מִמָּוֶת
הֲלֹא רַגְלַי מִדֶּחִי
לְהִתְהַלֵּךְ לִפְנֵי אֱלֹהִים
בְּאוֹר הַחַיִּים.

For You have saved me from death,
O yes, my foot from stumbling,
that I may walk in the presence of God,
in the light of life.

(Psalm 56:14)

The seventh night of Hanukkah: . . . **are "re-entering"—stepping into the next phase of life**

נֵר־לְרַגְלִי דְבָרֶךָ
וְאוֹר לִנְתִיבָתִי.

A lamp unto my feet is Your word,
A light for my path.

(Psalm 119:105)

The eighth night of Hanukkah: . . . **are surviving—incorporating the illness into their lives and stories**

אוֹר זָרֻעַ לַצַּדִּיק
וּלְיִשְׁרֵי־לֵב שִׂמְחָה.
שִׂמְחוּ צַדִּיקִים בַּיהוָה
וְהוֹדוּ לְזֵכֶר קָדְשׁוֹ.

Light is sown for the righteous,
Radiant joy for the upright-at-heart.
O you righteous ones, rejoice in Adonai.
and offer thanks to Adonai's holy name!

(Psalm 97:11–12)

The Masks of Purim

DEBBIE PERLMAN *z"l*

Purim is the time of topsy-turvy, inside-out. It is the time of the contrary, when appearances are deceptive. We put on a mask and become Esther the heroine, or Vashti the vanquished, or Haman the unspeakable.

So with my illness and disability. I have many masks to wear: some I choose, some that are forced upon me, some that just happen. Who am I? Who do I want to be?

> In this central core of me,
> You mark my potentials;
> You ignite the spark of eternity
> You have placed within me.

> I sometimes forget, Eternal God,
> The me that lies buried beneath
> The faces I must wear,
> The duties I take for my own.

I am the rebellious patient, the demanding one who, hospitalized, questions every medication I am handed and criticizes the bedside manner of interns. I exact responses when the respiratory therapist changes the settings on my ventilator. But this mask is also the mask of the self-advocate. I am protecting myself.

> Uncover the center of me, O God;
> Polish it and smooth it
> Like old cherished silver
> Handed down from mother to daughter.

I am the self-sacrificer, wearing my mask of compliance. Because I am frightened that if I make too much tumult, I will, like Vashti, be forgotten, sent to the silence of unanswered buzzers and unreturned telephone calls. I am agreeable while fuming. I smile my thanks, and my mask smiles, too, while beneath I cry.

I sometimes forget, Spark Maker,
That I glow with Your light,
That I burn with passions
I am sometimes frightened to reveal.

I am the happy cripple. And I am happy. My physical, spiritual, and financial needs are met. Within the confines of the world I have created for myself, I am free. I have everything that money can buy. What I really want—a return to the freedom of a whole and healthy body—is beyond any means. But I have made an armistice with that. And if I sometimes snarl at the oxygen hose that trips me up, I still am here, loved and loving others. This mask smiles like Mona Lisa and underneath I wear my look of serenity. I am at peace.

Send fuel to these sparks,
That I might light a way to righteousness;
Let a steady wind fan these flames
That serve You in faithfulness.

Then will my mouth praise You
From the center of my being;
Then will I strip away artifice
To praise the Living God.

Haggadah for Healing

DR. SHERRY BLUMBERG

The impetus for this Haggadah came out of my personal experience with cancer surgery just before Passover. My family and I celebrated the seder at a big metropolitan hospital. At first we were thrilled that such a seder was provided for the patients and their families. However, the experience of the seder was so frustrating and alienating that on the second night, when I was alone in my hospital room, I found myself creating a different kind of Haggadah.

Not that the Rabbi wasn't learned, and not that it wasn't wonderful to have his explanations, but present at that seder were patients in wheelchairs, on drips, weakened, dying and frail. Most of the patients left before we even got to the blessing for matzah. Next to my family was a family whose father was—at that very moment—having brain surgery. (The twelve and a half year old son was wondering if his father would live to witness his Bar Mitzvah.) Across from us was a family who gathered around the grandfather who would not see "next year" in Jerusalem with them. Even I could only stay until the meal was to be served—my own strength faded after 1½ hours at 9:00 P.M.

Yet, not once during this seder did I hear a mention of the terrible pain, the illness, the hopes for healing. My husband and son remained as I was taken back to my room and they heard none in the second half either.

The second night, I began to imagine what could be done. As I read through the Haggadah myself, I imagined many additions. Later in the week I began to write and illustrate them. Through the sampling presented below, we share with you some of the texts that I created in the hopes that you (perhaps your congregants or loved ones) may find these meaningful when woven into your seder this year.

As you read them, as you use them, please consider adding your own. Some texts below are incomplete, inviting you to complete them. . . .

Livrakhah u'refuah shleimah—with blessings and wishes for a complete healing.

Before kiddush (the first cup of the evening) one might say:

- We begin by pouring the wine. I pour it for you, as you sit here next to me, and ask that you in turn pour it for the one next to you and so on.

- Think about how our cup of life is filled. What does God do for us? What do we do for each other?

- I hold the cup differently as well. I hold it with both hands, with the fingers entwined. One hand symbolizes the part of me that is in need of healing; the other the hand that heals. On this night of Passover, the two come together as we celebrate.

- Smell the wine or grape juice. Relish its sweetness. See its rich color. Hear the melody as we chant the blessing. Then, after we say the blessing we will drink deeply from our cup.

- Each of these acts symbolizes that we must drink deeply from our cup of life, aware of all of our senses. During this season of freedom we celebrate each drop of life. Each is precious and should be savored. We do not know what will be tomorrow.

To accompany the Four Questions:

The four questions are traditionally asked by the youngest child at the seder. Tonight, we add four other questions that each of us may be moved to ask.

- A person struggling with illness may ask . . .
  Why me? On this night as all others I wonder why me?

- A person who is the loved one of someone ill may ask . . .
  How can I help? On this night as all others, what can I do to
  bring comfort?

- A doctor or nurse may ask . . .
  Will I have the skills to help save lives and mend broken bodies? On this night and throughout my life, will I be able to
  heal?

- A community may ask . . .
  How can we create a haven of safety, a support system, and a
  place of true prayer for those whose lives revolve around illness
  and healing? On this night and all nights, how can we serve
  God and the Jewish people?

What are the questions you would ask on this night?

Maggid: Telling the Story

B'chol Dor Va'Dor . . . In every generation there is illness and disease.
Illness can be a form of slavery. Some of us are again in physical
bondage to bodily and mental ills that keep us from thinking that we
are or can be free. On Passover, as we commemorate our people's
deliverance from the physical bondage of Egyptian slavery, we need
also to "tell our story." Where does your story begin?

- "And he went down into Egypt, and sojourned there. . ."
  (Deuteronomy 26:5). What is your Egypt?

- "And the Egyptians ill-treated us, and afflicted us, and laid upon
  us hard burdens" (Deuteronomy 26:6). How are you afflicted?
  What are your burdens?

- "And the Eternal brought us forth out of Egypt with a mighty hand and an outstretched arm; with great terror and with signs and wonders" *(Deuteronomy 26:8).* What has been your journey towards healing and freedom? What has God done? What great terrors have you felt? What have been the signs and wonders?

The Three Symbols of Passover

We tell the story of Passover through our symbols: *pesah* (the Passover sacrifice), *matzah* (unleavened bread) and *maror* (bitter herbs). As we hold up the symbols tonight and explain their ritual meaning, let us hear what they mean in terms of our own lives.

- *Pesah* . . . this is the sacrifice that we make in our own lives to help those who are in need. For those whose illness is chronic, it may mean the sacrifice of certain life styles. For those whose illness is terminal, it may mean the sacrifice of some dreams never to be realized. What does it mean to you?

- *Matzah* . . . this symbolizes that which has been left undone in our lives as we struggle with illness, disease and the pains of daily living. It has been called the bread of affliction and the bread of redemption. What is left undone in your life? What is that can be both an affliction and a redemption? What does the *matzah* mean to you?

- *Maror* . . . *maror* is sharp and bitter. We eat it with *haroset,* the sweet. We remember that bitterness is a part of everyone's life. We also know that it can be an opportunity for a moment of sweetness. Our liberation from the bitterness of illness is like leaving *Mitzrayim* (Egypt): to be redeemed, we must open ourselves to vulnerability. Both take courage.

Dayenu

Dayenu is a song of gratitude. Each of its verses moves us from one stage of awareness to another. While no one step is truly sufficient, and while with each step we continue to seek more, still, we must not overlook the blessings that we encounter along the way, step by step.

Dayenu is traditionally composed of 15 stanzas, reminiscent of the 15 steps of ascent in the Temple. In this *dayenu* we give you but a few verses that are steps towards healing. We urge you to write your own verses. Like the *dayenu* of the Exodus . . . we begin with the mundane and move to the spiritual, trying to feel gratitude for whatever we have:

- If we were blessed with early diagnosis, but not with wise doctors, *dayenu*.

- If we were blessed with wise doctors but not with a hospital nearby, *dayenu*.

- If we were blessed with a hospital nearby but not with a warm and dedicated nursing staff, *dayenu*.

- If I couldn't enjoy seder in my own home, but could share it with those I love, *dayenu*.

- If I am not blessed with complete healing of my body, but I am blessed with a healing of my soul, *dayenu*.

At the end of the seder we might say:

Illness and Disease can be
either a fence or a gate.

As a fence, it divides, keeping
people either in or out.
While protection is important,
and may be necessary at times,
there is beauty on both sides.

As a gate, it joins,
opening up new vistas,
new friendships
and new knowledge.

Illness and Dis"ease"
are not what we would
have chosen for ourselves,
but they are what we have
in our or our loved ones' lives.
Let us learn to see the
gateways it provides
and to move through
them as the truly beautiful
images of God that we can be.

Next year in Jerusalem.
Next year may we all be free.

VII

RESOURCES

Books of Healing and Comfort and Other Print Resources

Address, Richard F., Marcia Hochman, Harriet H. Rosen, and Anne Staffin. *Becoming a Kehilat Chesed: Creating and Sustaining a Caring Congregation.* New York: UAHC Press, 2002.

Beilenson, Evelyn L., ed. *First Aid for the Jewish Soul.* White Plains, N.Y.: Peter Pauper Press, 2000.

Bell, Yitzhack Leib, ed. *Healing Leaves: Prescriptions for Inner Strength, Meaning and Hope: From the Letters of Reb Noson of Breslov.* Deerfield Beach, Fla.: Simcha Press, 2000.

Benson, Herbert. *Timeless Healing: The Power and Biology of Belief.* New York: Scribners, 1996.

Blumberg, Sherry. "Haggadah for Healing." *The Outstretched Arm* 5, no. 2 (spring 1996): 4–5.

Cousins, Norman. *Head First: The Biology of Hope.* Farmington Hills, Mich.: Thorndike Press, 1990.

D'Augelli, Anthony R., Judith Frankel, and Steven J. Danish. *Helping Others.* Stamford, Conn.: Brooks/Cole Publishing Co., 1981.

Dossey, Larry, M.D. *Healing Words: The Power of Prayer and the Practice of Medicine.* San Francisco: HarperSanFrancisco, 1993.

Drown, Barbara. *New Mind New Body.* New York: Harper and Row, 1975.

Freeman, David, and Judith Abrams. *Illness and Health in the Jewish Tradition: Writings from the Bible to Today.* Philadephia: Jewish Publication Society, 1999.

Grollman, Earl, ed. *In Sickness and in Health.* Boston: Beacon Press, 1987.

Grosskopf, Barry. *Forgive Your Parents, Heal Yourself.* New York: Free Press, 1999.

Hall, Lindsey, and Leigh Cohn. *Bulimia: A Guide to Recovery.* Carlsbad, Calif.: Gurze Books, 1999.

Health and Healing. New York: Lilith Publications.

Hill, Karen. *Helping You Helps Me: A Guide Book for Self-Help Groups.* Ottawa: Canadian Council on Social Development, 1984.

Hoffman, Lawrence A. "From Common Cold to Uncommon Healing." *CCAR Journal* (spring 1994): 1–30.

Jaffe, Hirshel, ed. *Gates of Healing.* New York: Central Conference of American Rabbis, 1988.

Kay, Alan. *A Jewish Book of Comfort.* Northvale, N.J.: Jason Aronson, 1993.

Keeler, Bob. "Healing and Judaism." *Newsday,* May 7, 1996, B4–B5.

Klagsbrun, Francine. *Voices of Wisdom.* New York: Jonathan David, 2001.

Klein, Charles. *How to Forgive When You Can't Forget: Healing Our Personal Relationships.* New York: Berkley Books, 1997.

Koile, Earl. *Listening as a Way of Becoming.* Sacramento, Cal.: Regency Books, 1977.

Kushner, Harold. *When Bad Things Happen to Good People.* New York: Schocken, 1981.

LeShan, Eda. *When a Parent Is Very Sick.* Boston: Little, Brown, 1986.

Levine, Aaron. *How to Perform the Great Mitzvah of Bikkur Cholim.* Willowdale, Ontario: Zichron Meir Publications, 1987.

Levine, Stephen. *Healing into Life and Death.* Garden City, N.Y.: Anchor Books, 1987.

Levy, Naomi. *To Begin Again: The Journey Toward Comfort, Strength, and Faith in Difficult Times.* New York: Ballantine, 1999.

Life Lights: Help for Wholeness and Healing. Woodstock, Vt.: Jewish Lights, 2000.

Liss-Levinson, William S. *Hospice and the Synagogue Community.* Newsletter No. 13, fall 1986, Task Force on Bikur Cholim.

Litapayach Tikvah: To Nourish Hope—Eating Disorders: Perceptions and Perspectives in Jewish Life Today. New York: Union of American Hebrew Congregations Department of Jewish Family Concerts/UAHC Youth Division/Women of Reform Judaism, 2001.

McClure, Cynthia Rowland. *The Monster Within: Overcoming Bulimia.* Grand Rapids, Mich.: Fleming H. Revell, 2002.

Olitzky, Kerry M. *Jewish Paths toward Healing and Wholeness: A Personal Guide to Dealing with Suffering.* Woodstock, Vt.: Jewish Lights, 2000.

Out of the Depths: Personal Stories of Illness and Healing. New York: National Center for Jewish Healing, 1995.

Perlman, Debbie. *Flames to Heaven: New Psalms for Healing and Praise.* Wilmette, Ill.: Rad Publishers, 1998.

Pomerantz, Sharon. "Hospital of the Spirit." *Hadassah Magazine* 78, no. 3 (Nov. 1996): 45–47.

Remen, Rachel Naomi. *Kitchen Table Wisdom: Stories That Heal.* New York: Riverhead Books, 1996.

Rosenblum, Daniel, M.D. *A Time to Hear and a Time to Help.* New York: Simon and Schuster, 1991.

Rosman, Steven. *Jewish Healing Wisdom.* Northvale, N.J.: Jason Aronson, 1997.

Siegel, Bernie S., M.D. *Love, Medicine and Miracles.* New York: Harper and Row, 1986.

Spiegel, David, M.D. *Living Beyond Limits: New Hope and Help for Facing Life-Threatening Illness.* New York: Times Books, Random House, 1993.

Staudacher, Carol. *A Time to Grieve: Meditations for Healing after the Death of a Loved One.* San Francisco: HarperSanFrancisco, 1992.

Summers, Barbara Fortgang. *Community and Responsibility in the Jewish Tradition.* New York: United Synagogue of America, 1978.

Weintraub, Simkha Y., ed. *Healing of Soul, Healing of Body.* Woodstock, Vt.: Jewish Lights, 1994.

Weintraub, Simkha Y., with Aaron M. Lever. *Guide Me Along the Way: A Spiritual Companion for Surgery.* New York: National Center for Jewish Healing, 2001.

Winawer, Sidney J., M.D. *Healing Lessons.* Boston: Little, Brown, 1997.

Wolpe, David. *The Healer of Shattered Hearts: A Jewish View of God.* New York: Penguin Books, 1990.

Women of Reform Judaism. *Covenant of the Heart: Prayers, Poems and Meditations from the Women of Reform Judaism.* New York: WRJ, 1993.

Women of Reform Judaism. *Covenant of the Soul: New Prayers, Poems and Meditations from the Women of Reform Judaism.* New York: WRJ, 1997.

Organizational Resources

A Guide to Services of Jewish Healing. Ansche Chesed, 251 West 100th Street, New York, N.Y. 10025.

A Guide for Friendly Visiting. Dorot, Inc.

"Handholders" (providing personal care and attention to women having abortions). Main Line Reform Temple Sisterhood, Wynnewood, Pa.

"*Mi Shebeirach*—Healing of Mind, Healing of Body." WRJ District 22, Texas-Oklahoma Federation of Temple Sisterhoods.

National Center for Jewish Healing. *When the Body Hurts, the Soul Still Longs to Sing* (a prayerbook of blessings). New York: National Center for Jewish Healing, 1992.

National Center for Jewish Healing. *A Leader's Guide to Services and Prayers of Healing.* New York: National Center for Jewish Healing, 1996.

National Center for Jewish Healing. *The Outstetched Arm* (Newsletter of NCJH-To subscribe, call 212-399-2320). Also available, *Mi Sheberakh* card and *Evening and Morning: A Circle of Prayer* (a *bikkur cholim* card).

"Reflections" (a one-day retreat to nurture mind, body, and spirit). Temple Beth Orr Sisterhood, Coral Springs, Fla.

"*R'fua Sh'leima:* Jewish Women and Health in the 90's." Temple Isaiah Sisterhood, Lexington, Mass.

"SOS and Psychiatric Help Project." The Amsterdam Sisterhood, Amsterdam, Holland.

"Support Groups: Women in Pain Seeking Healing." WRJ District 22, Texas-Oklahoma Federation of Temple Sisterhoods.

Directory of Resources for Breast Cancer Patients and Their Families. UJA-Federation.

"*Yachad:* A Jewish Spiritual Support Group for Women with Breast or Ovarian Cancer." WRJ Sisterhood of Temple Beth-El of Great Neck, Great Neck, N.Y.

See also *The Or Ami Book* published for each Women of Reform Judaism Assembly, which highlights other programs of caring and service created by WRJ Sisterhoods.

The National Center for Jewish Healing can be reached in the following ways:
c/o JBFCS
850 Seventh Ave., Suite 1201
New York, New York 10019
Publications Phone 212-399-2320 Ex 216
General Info 212-399-2320 Ex 209
Fax 212-399-2475

Videos and Audiotapes

Dying to Be Thin. Films for the Humanities and Sciences (206) 382-3587.

Eating Disorders: The Hunger Within. Films for the Humanities and Sciences (206) 382-3587.

Friedman, Debbie. *Jewish Healing Video.* Renewal of Spirit Foundation, Miami Beach, Fla.

Zimmerman, Rabbi Sheldon. *Beyond the Misheberach: Creating a Service of Healing in the Synagogue.* Refaeinu Conference, 1994, The National Center for Jewish Healing, New York. Audiotape.

Web Sites

Bay Area Jewish Healing Center
www.growthhouse.org/ruachami.html

clickonJudaism.org
www.clickonJudaism.org

National Eating Disorders Association
www.nationaleatingdisorders.org

Harvard Eating Disorders Center
www.hedc.org

HealingPsalm.com/Debbie Perlman
www.healingpsalm.com

Jewish Healing Center (San Diego)
www.jfssd.org/JFSGrpsHealing.html

Jewish Link
www.geocities.com/JewishLink

National Center for Jewish Healing
www.jhhrn.org

Ohr Hadash Jewish Healing Center
members.tripod.com/JewishHealingCenter/

Washington Jewish Healing Network
www.washingtonjewishhealing.org

Music

"MiSheberach." Debbie Friedman. Sounds Write Productions.
"MiSheberach" and "Ruach Elohim." Lisa Levine. Transcontinental Music.
"Prayers for Healing." In *Cantor's Lifecycle Manual,* edited by B. Maissner, L. Levine, and M. Shochet. New York: American Conference of Cantors, 2000.
Refuah Shelema: Songs of Jewish Healing. New York: Synagogue 2000/Transcontinental Music, dist.